WILDFLOWERS 2

SAGEBRUSH COUNTRY

BY RONALD J. TAYLOR
AND ROLF W. VALUM

The Touchstone Press
P. O. Box 81
Beaverton, Oregon 97005

Library of Congress
Catalog Card No. 74-76843
I.S.B.N. No. 0-911518-26-6
Copyright© 1974
Ronald J. Taylor and Rolf W. Valum

This book is dedicated to George G. Taylor (father of the senior author), who was born, played, worked, and died within the limits of the sagebrush steppe. He was a man who appreciated the varied beauty and tranquility of nature, a man who loved the great outdoors as he loved life itself.

ACKNOWLEDGMENTS

In completing this work, extensive reference has been made to various floras and other botanical treatments dealing with those plants growing within the rather arbitrary geographical limits of *Sagebrush Country*. As much as possible, the comprehensive flora, *Vascular Plants of the Pacific Northwest* (Vol. 1-5) by Hitchcock, Cronquist, Ownbey, and Thompson, has been used as the primary authority on descriptive and distributional information. The design and preparation of illustrations was done by Dorothy Bird.

On the domestic front we acknowledge with appreciation the tolerance and patience that has been shown by our wives, Gloria Taylor and Darlene Valum, to our many absences associated with the study, collection, and photography of sagebrush steppe plants. We are especially grateful to Gloria who has spent hours reading and typing the manuscript.

R. J. T.
R. W. V.

Upper limits of Sagebrush steppe—West-Central Colorado

PROLOGUE

Sagebrush country is a land of contrasts, a desolate waste area or a place of beauty. It is a lifeless, lonely wilderness or an active world teeming with insects, vertebrates, and plant life. The winters are cold and are characterized by biting wind and blowing snow; summer days are uncomfortably hot but pass rather quickly into cool nights with clear, starry skies. Because of the winter cold and summer drought, a large part of the sagebrush zone has been called a cold desert. Still, occasional thunderstorms drench the cracked soil and rejuvenate the dormant plant life. The topography of the land is equally variable, ranging from sandy plains or alkaline flats to rugged rock formations and steep mountain slopes. The topographic pattern also influences the nature of the soil which may be deep and fertile or, more frequently, shallow and rocky.

To many people sagebrush country represents a "nothing" land, a dusty world of sand and tumbleweeds lying between the scattered towns of the west that represent civilization. To others sagebrush country is a fantasy land rich in legend and marked with romanticism attributable to the American cowboy of storybook, movie, and television fame. Yet, there is a real beauty for those who seek it, beauty expressed in colorful spring and fall flowers and more subtly in the wondrous adaptations which the plants and animals have undergone enabling them to withstand the extremes so typical of the sagebrush steppe. There is also enjoyment in being a part of sagebrush country, in camping under the stars with the ever-present smell of sage, listening for the eerie howl of the ubiquitous coyote, and being keenly aware of the "aloneness" so closely associated with the wide open spaces which have played such a truly great role in determining our American heritage.

CONTENTS

INTRODUCTION

As treated in this book, sagebrush country, or more accurately the sagebrush steppe, includes the major part of northern Nevada and adjacent California, eastern Oregon and Washington, southern Idaho, western Montana, northern Utah, much of Wyoming and the foothills and valleys of northwestern Colorado. A large portion of this vast region, especially Nevada, Utah, and southern Wyoming, constitutes the northern part of the Great Basin; and in discussions of plant distribution has often been referred to as such. Sagebrush itself extends well beyond these rather arbitrary limits, however, and may occur as the dominant member of local communities on the more moist northern slopes of desert mountains of California and the southern Rockies or in the winter-chilled, wind-swept plains of western Canada. Although this book does not characterize these outlying communities or include pictures and descriptions of associated plants found there, the vegetation is much like that of the steppe proper.

The community concept has been used rather extensively in this book and relates to a more or less repeatable association of plants, including dominants — those plants that exert the greatest influence because of size and/or density — and subordinates or simply associates. The community is normally named in honor of dominant species.

Sagebrush communities are indeed very widespread in the American west, as indicated above, but they are much more limited in distribution than is often thought. This is so because many shrubs of the steppes and deserts closely resemble sagebrush with casual observation from a speeding vehicle. Regularly spaced shrubs with a low symmetrical profile constitute a major part of the dominant vegetation from the Mojave Desert north through the sagebrush steppe and east into southern Utah and Colorado. Another problem with defining the limits of the sagebrush steppe or identifying sagebrush communities relates to other, often very closely related species of *Artemisia*. If these species as a group are considered to be sagebrush, then sagebrush in the broad sense becomes more widely distributed and ecologically more diverse. In this book sagebrush has been treated more or less in the broad sense, but certainly *Artemisia tridentata*, tall sagebrush, is the most widespread, the most common, and the most ecologically important of the several species.

Considerable vegetative diversity exists over the vast geographical area treated here as "sagebrush country" or the sagebrush steppe. In the southern extreme, particularly in central Nevada, there is extensive overlap between the steppeland with sagebrush-dominated communities and the northern, upland extension of the Mojave Desert with its more drought-tolerant plant types such as species of *Atriplex* (shadscale or saltbrush). Here the plant communities are relatively simple with few conspicuous dominants and a sparsity of associated species. In the foothills and high plains, the sagebrush steppe contacts and becomes interspersed with woodland communities, piñon pine and juniper in the south, juniper and/or mount mahogany in the north and east. In some areas, particularly in Idaho and Washington, the sagebrush steppe comes into direct contact with ponderosa pine or Douglas fir forests. Here the transition between forest and steppe is abrupt and isolated sagebrush communities occur on dry, south-facing slopes in otherwise forested regions. At the higher and northern limits of the sagebrush steppe, the lack of soil moisture is less critical and consequently the associated vegetation tends to be very lush with numerous representative species.

Over this broad geographical steppeland region of western North America, variable in climate, topography, and species, the single most important unifying characteristic is the presence of sagebrush, usually conspicuous and often a major dominant.

Vegetative Zones

Within a given area, such as the sagebrush steppe, the vegetation follows a pattern of distribution or zonation determined in large part by the physical and chemical properties of the soil. In this book six vegetative zones are recognized, although this represents an over-simplification. These zones are by no means absolute and the distribution of species within them is inconsistent from location to location. Still, each zone represents a pattern of vegetative uniformity both in species and plant form; and it is possible to relate most of the steppeland species to one of these six zones.

"Standard-type" zone — This zone is characterized by a lack of extremes. The soil is moderately deep, somewhat sandy and/or gravelly, usually slightly alkaline and sufficiently moist to support tall sagebrush *(Artemisia tridentata)* and various grasses, the two most prevalent plant-types. In the more moist sites, particularly near the forest margins, bitter brush *(Pursia tridentata)* communities are representative. Common associates of these communities include sagebrush, grasses, lupines, and balsamroots *(Balsamorhiza* species). In somewhat drier, sandy sites, species of rabbit brush

(Chrysothamnus) are extremely common and have similar associates. Other conspicuous dominants of the standard-type zone include several species of desert buckwheat (Eriogonum). Less common but colorful associates include species of Indian paintbrush (Castilleja), penstemon (Penstemon), larkspur (Delphinium), phlox (Phlox), desert parsley (Lomatium), locoweed (Astragalus), several daisies (Erigeron), and various liliaceous plants including wild onions (Allium), death camas (Zygadenus), and brodiaea (Brodiaea).

The standard-type zone is by far the most productive of the various vegetative zones (meadows excluded). A large part of this zone is under cultivation, particularly in areas of deep soil with the capability for irrigation. Most of the remainder is utilized to varying degrees for livestock grazing. With extreme grazing pressure, the natural vegetation is replaced by weedy, less palatable plant species. Unfortunately much of the sagebrush steppe has been overgrazed and thus altered, in some cases irreversibly so.

Lithosol zone—Lithosol by definition means rock-soil and this zone is thus characterized. Most lithosols occur in areas of basalt, accumulated from previous lava flows. Soil deposition is insignificant and primarily restricted to cracks in the basalt. Yet, because of the undesirable environmental conditions, rather than in spite of them, the lithosols provide some of the most spectacular arrays of spring flowers to be found in the sagebrush steppe. The more competitive plants, such as tall sagebrush and dominant grasses, are unable to withstand the rigors of the lithosols and cannot, therefore, crowd out the less competitive but more environmentally tolerant lithosol species.

Most lithosol species are low in stature and resemble the cushion plants of the arctic and alpine tundra. This adaptation provides the plants with protection against extreme water loss resulting from the hot sun and drying wind. Water is of course a major limiting growth factor in the lithosol zone and by midsummer the plants have become dormant with few signs of life.

The most important species of lithosols are rock sagebrush (Artemisia rigida), species of desert buckwheat (Eriogonum), and dwarf goldenweed (Haplopappus acaulis). Common, showy spring flowering associates include phlox (Phlox hoodii), rock penstemon (Penstemon gairdneri), daisies and other members of the sunflower family, and a few cacti. Low grasses also occur but are not dominants.

Sand (dune) zone—The soil of the sagebrush steppe tends to be sandy, and it is often difficult to draw the line between what might be called a dune area and the more sandy element of the standard-type zone. Still the distinction does exist and is reflected by the representative vegetation. In the dune zone, the sand tends to move thus creating an unstable condition and selecting for those plants which can tolerate shifts in sand depth. These plants normally have horizontal stems which produce upright shoots, or they have the capability to regenerate from lateral buds as the sand deposition increases. A deficiency of nitrogen is also characteristic of dune areas. Therefore, only those plants which can provide (fix) their own nitrogen, such as lupines and other legumes, or those which can tolerate nitrogen deficiencies are able to become established. Sand inhabitants of the latter group include sand dock (Rumex venosus), dune primrose (Oenothera pallida), Indian rice grass (Oryzopsis hymenoides), and a few short-lived annuals such as dune monkey flower (Mimulus nanus). As the sand becomes more stabilized, rabbit brush and other "sand-loving" species of the standard-type zone become established providing a mixture of vegetation from the two intergrading zones.

Talus zone—Numerous rock outcroppings, hills, and canyons occur in the sagebrush steppe. In many cases the slopes of these topographic irregularities are covered by rather coarse gravel or boulders. These talus slopes tend to be unstable because of gravitational movement of rock and this favors a particular combination of plant types, mostly large shrubs such as serviceberry (Amelanchier alnifolia) and wild (squaw) currant (Ribes cereum). In fine-gravelled talus there are a number of small, low shrubs or "subshrubs" including the beautiful and conspicuous purple sage (Salvia dorrii), Oregon sunshine (Eriophyllum lanatum), species of penstemon, desert buckwheat (Eriogonum), and evening primrose (Oenothera). Most talus shrubs, particularly the larger ones, require comparatively large amounts of water which they get from channeled drainage of precipitation through the rock system.

As a talus slope becomes stabilized by the establishment of vegetation, splintering of rocks, and deposition of wind-blown soil, many herbaceous species, such as lupines, invade the area to develop a lush community of mixed vegetation. This slow process of geological and vegetational change ultimately results in the conversion to a standard-type soil zone with the establishment of the dominant sagebrush and grasses and subsequent elimination of most talus species.

Meadow zone — In the high sagebrush plains, the drainage pattern is such that meadows are often formed in low depression areas. These meadows are, of course, characterized by year-round wet conditions. The vegetation is not at all similar to that of drier sites and includes many species of sedge *(Carex),* rushes *(Juncus),* some grasses, and a few very attractive flowering plants such as wild iris *(Iris)* and camas *(Camasia).* Various willows *(Salix)* are usually present in or around meadows, often forming dense thickets and providing shelter for associated animals.

A very restricted and meadowlike type of vegetative community is that of seepage areas. These areas occur most frequently along rock ledges below forested regions, and provide a brilliant rock gardenlike display of wild flowers. Some of the most common and widespread representatives are yellow monkey flower *(Mimulus guttatus),* shooting star *(Dodecatheon),* and a number of wild saxifrages.

Saline zone — With the weathering of rocks, calcium carbonates, sodium salts and other alkaline inducing compounds are released. In areas of low precipitation these compounds are not leached from the soil but accumulate thus resulting in somewhat saline conditions. If the parent rock is especially rich in soluble salts, the soil becomes so saline that only salt tolerant species can grow. These species (halophytes) have high internal concentrations of salts which allows them to withdraw water from salty soils whereas other plants could not and would perish from dehydration. Most salt-tolerant plants are non-showy shrubs of the Goosefoot family (Chenopodiaceae), and the most common representatives from the sagebrush steppe are hop sage *(Grayia spinosa),* winter fat *(Eurotia lanata),* and greasewood *(Sarcobatus vermiculatus).*

In many areas of the steppe the water table is near the surface and shallow ponds or lakes form during wet periods. Here the water remains until it evaporates leaving a salty residue. These low areas are termed "playas" or salt flats and are inhabited by a few extremely salt tolerant species which include saltbrush or shadscale *(Atriplex* species), greasewood and saltgrass *(Distichylis stricta).*

Adaptations

Since water is the major limiting factor of plant growth and reproduction in the sagebrush steppe, the plants have evolved a combination of adaptations which enable them to cope with the drought conditions.

These adaptations are numerous and varied but can be grouped into three general categories: 1) Those that enable plants to tolerate drought; 2) Those that assist the plants in avoiding drought; 3) Those that enable plants to escape drought altogether.

Adaptations leading to *drought tolerance* are physiological in nature and are typical of desert species. Some enable plant tissue to undergo extreme dehydration without permanent cell damage, others make it possible for the plants to extract water from very dry soil.

Drought avoidance is brought about by structural modifications which enable the plant to retain or conserve water. Common adaptations of this type include: 1) Thick cuticle — a waxy coating of the stems and leaves which is highly impervious to water. 2) Pubescence — hairiness which reduces evaporation from leaf surfaces by inhibiting air movement across the leaves and by reflecting sunlight, thus having a cooling effect. 3) Succulence—water storage tissue which provides vital water during periods of drought. 4) Low ratio of leaf surface to volume — small thick leaves, round leaves, rolled leaves, folded leaves, all modifications which cut down on evaporative area. 5) Internal leaf anatomy—there are numerous modifications of cell type and arrangement which help to reduce transpiration (loss of water vapor) and which guard against structural leaf damage resulting from excessive wilting.

Drought escaping plants are those which either have a persistent water supply or carry out their entire life cycle during the moist time of year. The latter group of plants, annuals, are extremely common in the steppe. They survive the dry periods in the form of seeds.

THE WHYS AND WHEREFORES
OF PLANT NAMES

Man is a rational animal who consciously or subconsciously strives toward the elimination of disorganization and confusion from his life. This has naturally led to the categorization and naming of all manner of things, since a name is necessary for efficient communication, a means by which we can converse without elaborate and detailed description. Problems of communication continue to exist, however, since names tend to be regional. The broader the distribution of a species, the greater the number of common names applied to that species. In an attempt to eliminate the ambiguities associated with the use of common names, botanists have adopted a set of rules and regulations leading to the acceptance of a single name for each species—the scientific or Latin name, a binomial consisting of the genus and species. Still, communication problems persist because of the inability to identify with a foreign sounding name with no obvious meaning. Considering these difficulties, the common names have been used extensively in this book, with Latin names providing for accuracy of identification. It must be emphasized, however, that the common name given here may be only one of several, the one most widely used or considered most appropriate.

What is in a name? The Latin binomial (two-names) consists of a noun (the genus or generic name) and a descriptive adjective (the species or, more accurately, the specific epithet). The generic name may be descriptive in nature or it may be given in honor of a person or place. Many originated in antiquity, especially with the ancient Greeks. The specific epithet although generally descriptive, may also be given in honor of a person or place, in which case it is written in an adjectival form.

Thus, there is meaning in the Latin binomial. It is descriptive and informative but, unfortunately, only to the individual with a knowledge of Latin and an appreciation for ancient Greek and Roman and early American history. It is not surprising, therefore, that people tend to be "turned-off" by Latin names and insist on using a common name which serves the same function but on a regional basis. Such names may be descriptive, for example "yellow bell" or "tumbleweed"; may relate to a habitat or location such as "desert paintbrush" or "Oregon sunshine"; or may have seasonal or diurnal significance, such as "spring beauty" and "evening primrose." Some names reflect a use, for example "winterfat." Finally, many common names are direct translations for the Latin, such as "balsamroot" from *Balsamorhiza.*

IDENTIFICATION AND ORGANIZATION OF REPRESENTATIVE SPECIES

To assist in the identification of steppe plants, a family key has been provided (Appendix I). This key has been kept as simple as possible, but its usage requires recognition of major plant parts and their variant forms. Reference to the descriptive illustrations and glossary will help in this respect. Keys for the identification of individual species have not been provided because they would necessarily be rather technical and the plants included in this book represent a small percentage of those occurring in the sagebrush steppe. Thus, identification of a plant will require a search through the pictures and descriptions of a chosen family, and, if the plant has been considered sufficiently common, attractive, or otherwise interesting to be included in this book, it should be possible to make a positive identification.

The various families of plants have been arranged in a standardized sequence which reflects the evolutionary relationships of flowering plants based on the opinions of some leading botanists of the late 19th century. Although many of their ideas are now known to be erroneous, their system is used in most floras and herbaria in the interest of consistency. In this book the species have been grouped within the families according to relationships. An exception to this is sagebrush which, although in the sunflower family, has been given a primordial position in the descriptive section. This is justifiable on the basis of its inclusion in the title of this book and its ecological importance in the steppes of North America.

Appendix II may also be of some value in identification of species or may otherwise be of some interest to the reader. In it, each species has been placed under the heading of the vegetative zone(s) in which it most frequently occurs. In the index, species have been listed alphabetically by common and scientific name.

Mosaic of spring flowers near Ellensburg, Washington

FAMILIES

SAGEBRUSH (Artemisia species)

The term sagebrush refers collectively to several species of low shrubs distributed throughout the semiarid regions of North America. Among these species, **tall sagebrush (Artemisia tridentata),** the state flower of Nevada, has the broadest ecological tolerance and thus can survive under the greatest range of environmental conditions. Still, it grows best in deep, relatively moist soils that are mildly basic (rather than acidic). Under such ideal conditions, individual plants may become very large and robust, up to 8 feet tall and equally broad through the branched crown. As the water availability decreases and soil conditions deteriorate, tall sagebrush becomes progressively smaller and in many dry, rocky areas may average less than 1 foot in height. Interestingly, the height and uniformity of growth can be used as a measure of cultivation potential assuming irrigation capabilities. If the plants average approximately 3 feet or more in height, the soil may be considered productively arable.

Tall sagebrush has evolved a number of adaptations "designed" to increase the efficiency of water absorption and retention under semiarid conditions. The leaves are small with a limited surface area from which water can be lost through transpiration. Also, they are densely covered with grayish hairs which further reduce transpiration, both by reflecting sunlight and therefore cooling the plant and by inhibiting the movement of dry wind across the leaf surface. Furthermore, the plants become somewhat dormant during the drier part of the year

Sagebrush

thus conserving water. "Rapid" growth resumes in the late winter and moist spring.

Tall sagebrush also has an efficient root system, consisting of small, widely dispersed, shallow roots which absorb water rapidly before it can evaporate following rainstorms, and coarse, penetrating roots which draw water from reservoirs deep beneath the earth's surface.

Although tall sagebrush has a broad ecological tolerance, it is not necessarily a strong competitor. In the more moist extremes of its ecological range it tends to be replaced by grasses and/or other shrubs, or even trees. However, the decay of its fallen leaves results in the release of toxic compounds that apparently limit the growth of some would-be competitors. Other environmental factors also influence competi-

tive ability. Under conditions of heavy grazing, competing grasses are depressed and sagebrush growth is therefore enhanced. In contrast, fire selectively destroys the dry, woody sagebrush plants favoring increased density of grasses.

The minute flowers of sagebrush are produced during late summer or early fall in numerous small yellowish heads. Although insect pollination tends to be the rule in most members of the sunflower family (Compositae), sagebrush is wind pollinated. This results in an allergic response and associated discomfort by some people, and this response is further aggravated by the slow flower production and consequent extension of the flowering period. The volatile chemicals which are responsible for the strong sage odor may also have a mild

Sagebrush

allergenic effect.

Among the most important identifying characteristics of tall sagebrush are leaf, shape and color. The grayish color attributable to dense hairs has previously been mentioned. The shape is wedgelike and, as the name "tridentata" indicates, three-lobed at the broadened tip. However, there are usually a number of more elongate, non-lobed leaves near the branch tips.

Another important species of the western steppeland (Washington, Oregon, Idaho, and Montana) is **rock sagebrush (Artemisia rigida)** which is a major dominant in dry, rocky (lithosol) areas. It is a low shrub (up to 2 feet tall) with deeply divided (rather than lobed) leaves and blackish stems and branches.

The genus was named in honor of Arte-misia, wife of Mausolus, ancient ruler of Caria (Southwest Asia Minor). Mausolus died in 353 BC and his bereaved wife perpetuated his memory by the erection of a magnificent monument — mausoleum — which became one of the seven wonders of the world. Artemisia herself was named in honor of the Greek goddess Artemis, the virgin huntress or goddess of wild nature.

Rock sagebrush

EPHEDRA FAMILY (Ephedraceae)

Green ephedra (Ephedra viridis)—Species of *Ephedra* are unusual in several aspects. They lack flowers and the seeds are produced in small conelike structures at the junctures of jointed stems. The leaves are reduced and occur as small bracts or scales, also at stem joints. The stems are green and photosynthetic with numerous stiff, upright, broomlike branches.

The various ephedras are widely distributed in the arid southwest, particularly in desert mountains of California, Nevada, and Utah, extending southward into Mexico. Green ephedra is widespread along the transitional zone between piñon-juniper woodlands and more xeric (drier) communities. In central Nevada its distribution widely overlaps with sagebrush, although it is more common further south in the Mojave Desert region.

The antidepressant and anticongestion drug ephedrine is a naturally occurring alkaloid in *Ephedra.* In spite of this, the stems have historically been dried and used as a source of a slightly pungent tea, thus the frequently applied common names of Mexican and Mormon tea.

Green ephedra

GRASS FAMILY (Gramineae)

The grasses constitute the single most important group of plants in the sagebrush steppe. They are indispensible as the major food source for nearly all herbivorous inhabitants, including cattle. They are dominant representatives of steppe communities and as such have a major influence on the structure of those communities. They are instrumental in preventing or inhibiting soil erosion and participate in the stabilization of dunes. They provide shelter for various small animals and serve a number of lesser roles. Like all large families, however, the Gramineae is not without its villains. Some of the most successful weeds are grasses. Many species produce "seeds" which become lodged in the mouths of grazing animals. Some intro- duced species are very aggressive and thrive in the steppe at the expense of native grasses and other plants. Finally, all grasses are "villains" in that they are wind pollinated and produce large masses of air-borne pollen over long periods of time. The respondents are, of course, the thousands of hay fever victims.

Strategies of adaptation exploited by grasses are both numerous and effective. The evolution of elaborate anatomical and structural characteristics has enabled grasses to absorb and conserve water efficiently. In addition, most species can tolerate extensive dehydration without permanent tissue damage. Finally, many species are short-lived annuals which are able to complete their life cycle (from seed to seed) during moist periods, thus *escaping* drought.

Grassland scene, northern Nevada

21

Unquestionably, there is no similarly large group of plants so well adapted to the semi-arid conditions of the steppe as are the grasses.

Grasses have also evolved an efficient system of wind pollination. The sepals and petals which can only interfere with the transfer of pollen by wind have been lost. At the time of pollen release, the stamens become elongate and extend well beyond confining bracts thus enabling the pollen to be freely dispersed by the wind. At the same time, the sticky, pollen receptive stigmas, with their numerous branches, become completely exposed and "comb" the air for pollen grains.

In spite of extensive and obvious differences among most species, grasses in general tend to look alike and there is some basis for the statement, "if you've seen one grass you've seen them all" or "a grass is a grass is a grass. . . ." The leaves are primarily basal and tufted, and are long, narrow, and parallel-veined. Stems are round and jointed, and are derived from extensively branched root systems or from creeping rhizomes (underground stems). The flowers consist only of stamens and/or pistils and are associated with various chafflike bracts which often have hairlike or bristlelike appendages (awns). The flower(s) and associated bracts are collectively referred to as a spikelet. Spikelets may be borne directly on the stem, as with wheat, or on flexuous branches, as with oats. The fruit is, of course, a grain.

Any comprehensive treatment of steppe vegetation would necessarily include dis-

Spiked wheatgrass

cussion of numerous species of grasses. However, only a few of the most important representatives are considered here.

Spiked wheatgrass (Agropyron spicatum) is one of the most important forage grasses of the steppe. It is a rather tall (up to 3 feet) bunch grass with numerous slender stems, each with a narrow terminal spike. It is common and often a conspicuous dominant in the more moist regions, particularly in areas of deep soil accumulation. Most of the wheatgrass prairies are now under cultivation.

Steppe bluegrass (Poa sandbergii) is one of several poorly distinguished bluegrasses. It forms small clumps with narrow, short leaves and slender stems with many small spikelets on short upright branches. It occurs on thinner, drier soils than spiked wheatgrass, often on lithosols.

Idaho fescue (Festuca idahoensis) resembles steppe bluegrass but is taller, occurs in larger clumps, has bristlelike awns in the spikelets, and is found in deeper, more moist soils, often in association with ponderosa pine.

Cheat grass (Bromus tectorum) is an introduced annual which has become distributed throughout the steppe. It competes successfully against native species, especially in over-grazed or otherwise disturbed areas. It is characterized by its rather large nodding spikelets with long, firm, bristlelike awns.

Indian rice grass (Oryzopsis hymenoides) is an attractive bunch grass with a diffusely branched, feathery crown. It is very important in the stabilization of dunes.

Steppe bluegrass

Cheat grass

23

Another grass which favors sandy soil is **needle grass (Stipa comata)** which has very long, twisted, needlelike awns.

Giant wild rye (Elymus cinereus) is a very coarse and tall (up to 6 feet) grass that occurs in large bunches, usually in relatively moist, slightly alkaline flats. It has dense spikes and in this respect resembles wheat. In salt flats, it is replaced by the low, **creeping salt grass (Distichlis stricta).**

In Colorado and the eastern extreme of the sagebrush zone, the **blue gramma (Bouteloua)** and **buffalo (Buchloe)** grasses become the most important range grasses. These two species do not form clumps as do bunch grasses, but spread by runners or rhizomes. Both grasses are attractive and have the spikelets concentrated on one side of the spike.

Indian rice grass

Giant wild rye

LILY FAMILY (Liliaceae)

Wild onion (Allium species) — Wild onions are both numerous and generally difficult to distinguish. All are herbaceous plants with basal, grasslike leaves and round or elongate bulbs. The flowers are borne in an attractive umbrella- or head-like cluster at the tip of the stem. Each flower has a combination of three petals and three sepals which are more or less similar in shape, size, and color. Occasionally, the flowers are replaced by small bulbs.

The various wild onions are widespread and frequently form dense populations which are very showy during the flowering season, with their pink to purple or white colors. Like cultivated onions the wild forms are easily recognized by their onion- or garlic-like odor from which the genus gets its name (Latin: *allium* = garlic). All species are edible and can be used to make excellent garlic butter or as a flavor additive to wild game.

The most common and widespread of the wild onions is **Allium acuminatum** which occurs more or less throughout the sagebrush steppe. The flower color is somewhat variable but is most frequently rose-purple. A widespread white-flowered species is **Allium textile** which is common in the eastern "half" of the steppeland. A very attractive pink flowered species is **A. douglasii** of eastern Oregon and Washington.

Brodiaea (Brodiaea douglasii) — With the exception of some of the wild onions, this species is the most widespread and populous lily of the sagebrush steppe. It is also common in piñon-juniper woodlands,

Wild onion (A. acuminatum)

Wild onion (A. textile)

Brodiaea (B. douglasii)

25

in open ponderosa pine forests, and along rocky, montane ridges.

Although the flowers of brodiaea are showy, the plants themselves are unattractive. Each has a deeply buried, flattish, fibrous-coated bulb; a tall (up to 3 feet), thin, flexuous stem with an umbrellalike cluster of several flowers; and one or two grasslike leaves which are nearly as long as the stem and are borne from the bulb below ground level. The flowers vary in color from pale to dark blue and are fused at the base to form a tube with six lobes (petals), each with wavy margins.

Two additional species of *Brodiaea* occur in the steppeland. These are **B. howellii,** a frequent plant along the western "edge" of the steppe, and **B. hyacinthina,** an occasional plant in the western "half" of the steppe. Both have whitish, or pale blue flowers and in the latter species the floral tube is much shorter than the lobes. All three brodiaeas "prefer" relatively deep, sandy soils in moderately dry sites.

Like those of onions, the bulbs of brodiaea are edible and were eaten extensively by Indians and early settlers. Unlike onions, however, brodiaea bulbs have a nutlike flavor when cooked.

Camas (Camassia quamash)—Camas is a beautiful plant with large and congested, pale to dark blue flowers. As is true of most lilies, the sepals and petals are alike in color and size (about 1 inch long), and the flower parts are in multiples of three—three sepals, three petals, six stamens, and three compartments in the ovary. Stems are usually 1-2 feet tall, have a few fleshy, grasslike

Camas

leaves with parallel veins, and are derived from starchy bulbs.

The names "camas" and "quamash" were given to this plant by Indians who relied upon the bulbs as a source of food. Early settlers also used the bulbs as a food supplement, and even today they are regularly collected and eaten by some people including Indians, especially Nez Percé.

Camas grows in meadows or low, non-salty areas which are wet in the spring. Often it forms vast populations such as in the Camas Prairie near Lewiston, Idaho, which can be seen from the hills above as a sea of blue color during the spring flowering period. Camas has a wide range and is found in suitable habitats throughout western North America.

Death camas (Zygadenus venenosus)—

Death camas is a common associate of sagebrush over much of the steppeland. It is a typical liliaceous plant with long, rather thick, parallel-veined leaves and a slightly elongate bulb which progressively buries itself more deeply as the plant ages. The flowers are borne in a rather dense pyramidal cluster which becomes more elongate, and the individual flowers accordingly become more widely spaced, as flowering progresses. The sepals and petals are similar in number, three each, and both are white or more commonly cream-colored to pale yellow. The fruit develops into a three-lobed capsule.

For many years it has been known that death camas contains an alkaloid poisonous to livestock, particularly sheep. Also, people who have eaten the bulbs as a result of

Death camas

mistaken identity have suffered accordingly. An interesting aspect of the poisonous nature of death camas relates to its nectar. It has been demonstrated through experimentation that honeybees can be fatally poisoned from feeding on the nectar. It seems, therefore, that the poisonous property has created a conflict of interest for death camas.

Yellow bell (Fritillaria pudica)—One of the most unforgettable "characters" of "Sagebrush Country" is the beautiful yellow bell. Undoubtedly, its popularity relates in part to the fact that it flowers in very early spring when the desolate recesses of winter linger over the drab countryside. Frequent and colorful spring flowering associates of yellow bell are spring beauty (Claytonia lanceolata), salt and pepper (Lomatium gormanii), and steppe buttercup (Ranunculus glaberrimus).

Like other lilies, the floral parts of yellow bell occur in multiples of three and the sepals and petals are similar in color and form. The individual plants are derived from a bulb with numerous smaller grainlike bulblets. The leaves are elongate and fleshy and are borne in pairs or in whorls of three or more near midlength on the stem. The bright yellow, nodding, bell-shaped flowers are borne singly or in pairs at the stem tip and become orangish with age. The capsule bears a resemblance to a dice box and it is this likeness which is responsible for the generic name (Latin: *fritill* = dice box). *Pudica* is Latin for ashamed or bashful and must relate to the flower's nodding habit.

The yellow bell is common in the high

Yellow bell

plains and open forests of western North America, in areas with sufficient spring moisture. It is also common along rocky ridges in the mountains. Here, too, it is usually associated with sagebrush.

Mariposa or sego lily (Calochortus species)—As indicated by their Greek derivation *(Kalo* = beautiful, *chorta* = grass), the species of *Calochortus* are very attractive. They are well marked by their three broad, lavender to white petals which usually have a patch of hairlike filaments on the inner surface near the base and an associated purple band or splotch. The stems are unbranched below the flower stalks, bear a few to several rather thick but grasslike leaves and arise from round starchy bulbs. The flowers are typical of lilies with three sepals, three petals, six stamens, and a triangular (often winged) ovary that matures into a many-seeded capsule.

The showiest species is **mariposa lily (Calochortus macrocarpus),** a tall plant with 1-3 large, pale to dark lavender flowers. The sepals are narrow, approximately 2 inches in length, somewhat longer than the broad, greenish-striped petals. Mariposa lily occurs in dry sandy soil often in major river drainages.

A very common species in the eastern "half" of the steppeland is **sego lily (Calochortus nuttallii),** the state flower of Utah. It has a conspicuous red to purple band near the base of the 1-1½ inch long petals which are usually longer than the sepals. The sego lily is found in dry, sandy or rocky soil.

Mariposa lily

Sego lily

Cat's ears

IRIS FAMILY (Iridaceae)

Wild iris, flag (Iris missouriensis)—The wild iris is a strikingly beautiful plant that forms small but dense populations which spread by rootstalks (rhizomes). As the populations increase in diameter, the central, older individuals often die leaving an outer ring of plants. The stems are 1-2 feet tall and have several grasslike leaves of approximately equal height. The showy flowers have three drooping blue sepals (2-3 inches long), usually with purplish lines; three erect, somewhat smaller petals; and three blue style branches which are flattened and petallike. The fruit is a large capsule.

Wild iris grows in meadows or in low areas that are wet or moist in the spring but become very dry later in the year. They may be expected in suitable habitats throughout the steppeland. Sometimes when other food sources are unavailable, cattle feed on the leaves and stems of wild iris and are afflicted with a "belly-ache." The rootstalks, especially, contain a toxic material, irisin, which can be lethal if eaten. Plains Indians reportedly used this toxin in a mixture of bile as an arrowhead poison.

Iris is the Greek word for rainbow. Presumably this genus was given the name because of its showy flowers which occur in a variety of bright colors. In *Iris missouriensis* the flower color varies from a very pale blue to dark blue or bluish-purple.

Grass widow (Sisyrinchium species)—There are three species of grass widow (or blue-eyed grass) which have limited distribution in the sagebrush steppe. All have

Wild iris, flag

similar habitat requirements—moist spring conditions in the high plains or open forests—and all combinations apparently hybridize when their ranges overlap.

Grass widows flower early in the spring after which time they become "hidden"—because of their grasslike appearance—among the steppe vegetation. The flowers are borne singly or in small clusters on the flattened stems, at the base of one or more sheathing leaves. The flower parts occur in threes: three sepals, three petals, three stamens, and three compartments in the ovary.

The most widespread and variable of the grass widows is **Sisyrinchium angusti-folium** which has in the past been divided into a number of species. It has comparatively small, blue flowers and occurs spo-radically in suitable habitats throughout the steppeland and adjacent ponderosa pine forests and piñon-juniper woodlands. The most attractive species is **S. douglasii,** a grass widow with relatively large, purple flowers. This plant occurs in Washington, Oregon, and California. The third species, **S. inflatum,** is a similar but smaller-flowered plant which extends from the Cascade and Sierra Ranges to eastern Idaho and northern Utah.

Grass widow (S. douglasii)

WILLOW FAMILY (Salicaceae)
Quaking aspen (Populus tremuloides)
—Quaking aspen can hardly be considered to be an element of the sagebrush steppe; yet it frequently does occur in the high plains and foothills along ravines or well-drained depressions where seepage often occurs early in the spring and the water table remains near the surface through the dry summer months. In these areas water is made available primarily by large snow drifts which form along the crests of the hills above. However, in spite of a greater water availability here than in the surrounding sagebrush communities, these sites are rarely marshy nor are they meadowlike in aspect. The deep and fertile sandy-loam soil of the aspen groves results from years of erosion of the upland slopes. The most frequent associates of aspen are large shrubs: chokecherry, serviceberry and hawthorn, all of which produce edible fruit.

The aspen grove surrounded by a "sea" of sagebrush is an impressive sight. The trees are rather tall and straight with conspicuously white bark and dark green, trembling or quaking leaves. In the fall, the leaves of aspen and associated shrubs provide a splash of golden color which contrasts sharply with the gray-green hue of the surrounding sagebrush. The aspen grove is also a haven for birds and wildlife, providing food, sometimes water, and always shelter from insects, predators, man, and adverse environmental elements.

Several species of **willow (Salix)** grow in and around meadow areas. These are rather large shrubs, "pussy willows."

Quaking aspen

SANDALWOOD FAMILY (Santalaceae)
Bastard toad-flax (Comandra umbellata)

—Like its common name, this plant is rather unattractive. It is seldom more than 12 inches tall and the erect stems are derived in clumps from spreading root-stalks (rhizomes). Each stem has numerous alternate and elliptical gray-green leaves. The flowers are borne in a terminal flat-topped or rounded cluster. Petals are absent and the sepals vary in color from green to pale purplish. The ovary is inferior (borne below the sepals and stamens) and matures into a berrylike, blue, purplish, or brown fruit which is normally edible but may contain deleterious amounts of selenium which the plants accumulate if growing in selenium-rich soils.

Like several unrelated plants of the steppe, bastard toad-flax is a root parasite, extracting materials from a wide range of host plants. Although it is fully photosynthetic and apparently can survive without a host, its extremely wide range is undoubtedly due in part to its parasite-host relationship. It is distributed throughout the semi-arid region of western North America and is especially abundant in moderately sandy soils.

Bastard toad-flax

BUCKWHEAT FAMILY (Polygonaceae)
Desert buckwheat (Eriogonum species)
—As a group, desert buckwheats are among the most important dominants of the sagebrush steppe, second only to grass and sagebrush. Most species "prefer" gravelly or sandy soils and are often co-dominants of sagebrush communities; others are dominant members of rocky (lithosol) communities. All species are well adapted to withstand the summer drought.

With the exception of a number of mostly small and inconspicuous annuals, the steppe species of *Eriogonum* are long-lived perennials with branched woody stems and densely hairy, basal leaves. The flowers are individually very small and are derived (usually in dense, ball-like clusters) from cup-shaped structures (involucres) with toothed or lobed margins. The involucres with their flowers are borne singly or in umbrellalike groups at the end of upright, nearly leafless stems. Each flower has three sepals and three petals (considered by many scientists to be six sepals) which are usually similar in size, structure and color. The floral color varies among and within species from white or yellow to pink or reddish. The flowers persist for many days and tend to become darker colored (yellow-red) as they age.

The desert buckwheats are attractive plants, especially those with colorful, ball-shaped flower clusters. Most species flower in late spring or early summer, others in early spring, some in late summer. Collectively, they probably provide the single most important nectar source for steppe-inhabit-

Desert buckwheat (E. umbellatum)

34

ing bees. Seeds provide a major source of food for birds and rodents.

The most important and widespread species of desert buckwheat is **Eriogonum heracleoides** which occurs more or less throughout the steppe. This plant very frequently achieves dominant status in gravelly soils and on rocky ridges. It is shrubby at the base with narrow, densely hairy leaves. The flowering stems usually have a whorl of leaves near mid-length and another whorl below the several flowering stalks, each of which has one or more ball-like clusters of flowers. The floral color is usually whitish-yellow becoming reddish in age. Flowers are produced in early summer.

A highly variable and attractive species is **E. ovalifolium** which ranges from the sagebrush steppe to alpine ridges. It is a relatively low plant with many basal, oval, woolly leaves and a few to several leafless flowering stems each with a dense ball-shaped cluster of colorful white, reddish, or yellow flowers. It occurs in a wide range of habitats throughout the sagebrush steppe and is especially common through eastern Idaho, Wyoming, and the Great Basin. It flowers in early to mid summer.

Another extremely variable and wide-ranging species is **E. umbellatum** which can be found in a multitude of habitats from sagebrush steppe to alpine ridges. The flowers occur in two to six dense clusters and the color varies from white to bright yellow or pink to red. Flowering occurs in mid summer or earlier depending on elevation and exposure. The woody stems are extensively branched and often mat-form-

Desert buckwheat (E. heracleoides)

Desert buckwheat (E. ovalifolium)

ing. The upright, flowering stems have a whorl of leaves below the flower clusters. This is probably the most common species in the steppe of the Great Basin and adjacent Colorado.

An equally variable but less attractive species is **E. strictum** with whitish to pale yellow or pink flowers which are produced in early summer. The leaves are all basal, small, oblong, and densely hairy. The stems are branched above with few to several large or small clusters of flowers. This species is widely distributed throughout the western "half" of the steppeland, mostly in sandy plains.

A very colorful desert buckwheat is **E. compositum** with many clusters of usually bright yellow flowers borne in an umbrella-like pattern. The plants are well marked with their relatively large (often several inches), triangular or heart-shaped, densely white-woolly leaves. This plant has a limited distribution, occurring in rocky habitats of Washington, eastern Idaho, and northeastern Oregon. It flowers in early summer.

A very attractive, compact plant of basaltic soils (lithosols) of eastern Washington and Oregon and southwestern Idaho is **E. thymoides.** This nearly symmetrical cushion plant has numerous short upright branches each bearing a very dense cluster of yellow, whitish, or pink to rose-red flowers. The small petals or petal-like sepals are densely covered with long whitish hairs. The leaves are narrow, less than ½ inch long, are densely hairy, and are borne in whorls of several at the base and near mid-length of the upright flowering stems. This species

Desert buckwheat (E. strictum)

Desert buckwheat (E. compositum)

Desert buckwheat (E. thymoides)

flowers in the spring.

Another dominant and showy species of lithosol communities in the western "half" of the steppe is **E. sphaerocephalum** which flowers in early summer. This is a low extensively branched shrub with small (approximately 1 inch long) woolly (at least on the underside) leaves which are whorled at the ends of branches and below the flower clusters. The flowers are usually bright yellow and are borne in few to several clusters per stem.

A third desert buckwheat of rocky habitats is **E. caespitosum.** This plant forms very dense, low mats with numerous small (less than 1 inch long) oblong, hairy leaves and short upright flowering stalks, each bearing a single small cluster of yellow to reddish (with age) flowers. This species is widespread from Idaho and Montana east and south through the sagebrush steppe and onto Rocky Mountain ridges. It flowers in early summer.

Sand dock (Rumex venosus) — Sand dock is both unusual and attractive though it quickly deteriorates into an off-color "eye-sore." The plants spread by thick woody rootstalks (rhizomes) and often form dense populations. Upright stems are rather succulent and bear several broad and heavily-veined leaves which may be as much as 6 inches long. Above each leaf is a conspicuous papery sheath (sheathing stipule).

Desert buckwheat (E. sphaerocephalum)

Desert buckwheat (E. caespitosum)

Sand dock

GOOSEFOOT FAMILY (Chenopodiaceae)

Hopsage (Grayia spinosa)—Hopsage is a medium-sized, unisexual, shrub with a profile similar to that of sagebrush. The spiny stems are grayish and bear many elliptical leaves, about 1 inch long. The flowers are small and inconspicuous and consist of little more than stamens—in staminate (male) plants, or pistils—in pistillate (female) plants. However, as the seeds of the pistillate plants mature, each becomes enclosed by two enlarged bracts which vary in color from whitish or greenish to shades of red. Therefore, the pistillate plants become rather attractive as the two bracts develop.

Hopsage grows in a wide variety of habitats from talus slopes to alkaline flats, from dry sagebrush plains to the Mojave Desert.

It flowers in early spring but the fruits with their showy bracts do not achieve full color until early summer.

Grayia was named in honor of Dr. Asa Gray, one of the most renowned North American botanists. His *Flora of North America* still ranks high among taxonomic treatments. He was also a consultant to Sir Charles Darwin and a great 19th Century teacher.

Winter fat (Eurotia lanata)—This is an interesting though not particularly attractive shrub with many low, erect branches covered by white woolly or feltlike hairs. The generic name is derived from the Greek *euro* which means mold and refers to the "moldy," whitish coloration of the plants. *Lanata* is of Latin derivation and means wool. The flowers are small and appear as

Hopsage

Winter fat

balls of cotton in the axils of the short and narrow leaves.

Winter fat occurs in dry, salty or alkaline flats in the deserts and steppes of western North America. Usually it is associated with other salt-tolerant plants (halophytes) but often forms rather pure stands which are very conspicuous by the low stature and whitish color of the plants. It is a highly desirable browse plant and has been utilized by sheepmen as winter feed for their herds; hence the common name.

Greasewood (Sarcobatus vermiculatus) —Greasewood is a white-barked shrub that may grow to be several feet tall and is clearly distinct from sagebrush and most other steppe shrubs by its bright green— rather than grayish—foliage. The numerous small, linear leaves are succulent (Gr. sarco = fleshy) and roundish to triangular in cross-section. The many branches are spiny, thus the Greek suffix *batus* which means bramble. The inconspicuous flowers are unisexual, the staminate (male) occurring in small cone-shaped structures at the ends of small branches and the pistillate (female) occurring in the axils of leaves below the "cone".

Greasewood grows in alkaline flats and playas. It can tolerate excessive soil salts which would draw the water out of less-well adapted plants. Its ability to absorb and retain water in salty soils is dependent upon the accumulation of sodium salts in the leaf and root tissue. These salts are readily detectable by the taste of the fleshy leaves.

Greasewood often forms extensive populations in salt flats, with the exclusion of

Greasewood

almost all other vegetation. Usually it is found in areas where abundant ground water is available to its deeply penetrating root system. It is distributed throughout the sagebrush steppe and is an excellent indicator of alkaline soils.

Russian thistle, tumbleweed (Salsola kali)—Although Russian thistle is an introduction from Eurasia, it has now become established throughout the steppeland. It owes its distribution efficiency to its annual habit and circular growth form. When the plants die in the autumn, they break away from the roots and tumble freely in the wind scattering seeds as they go, often for many miles. Fortunately it is not an aggressive competitor and thus cannot replace native species but occurs along roadsides, fence lines, wheat field margins, overgrazed sites and other areas where the steppe communities have been disrupted. It is a remarkable plant in that it does all its growing during late summer when the water supply has essentially been depleted.

Russian thistle is truly a noxious weed, both because of its distributional pattern and its general spininess. It is an extensively-branched herbaceous plant with numerous narrow, needlelike, fleshy leaves and bracts, all rigid and spine-tipped. The stems and branches vary in color from green to red, often with darker stripes. The flowers are small and inconspicuous and are borne at the base of leaves and bracts. The petals (or sepals) are papery in texture and generally of the same color as the stems. The generic name is derived from the Latin *Salsus* meaning salty.

Russian thistle

Russian thistle

PURSLANE FAMILY (Portulacaceae)

Spring beauty (Claytonia lanceolata)—Although the spring beauty is more at home in mountain meadows and on alpine slopes, it is not uncommon in the high sagebrush plains. Here it occurs in areas of abundant spring moisture, usually as a result of concentrated run-off from melting snow fields. It often forms very dense populations and flowers within a few days of snow recession. It is indeed a "spring beauty."

The plants are mostly less than 6 inches tall with deeply buried bulbs and few to several weak, succulent, brittle stems, each bearing a pair of strongly veined, lance-shaped leaves. The flowers are produced in an elongate cluster (raceme) above the two leaves. Each flower has two green sepals, five white to, more often, pink (with darker stripes), notched petals, and five stamens. The bulbs are starchy and potatolike but reputedly have toxic properties unless cooked. Still, they have been widely gathered in the past as a food source.

Spring beauty

41

Bitterroot (Lewisia rediviva)—Bitterroot, or rock rose, is an unusual plant which grows along rocky ridges and in thin soils of basalt flats where it remains partially hidden among the rocks or in rock crevices until the beautiful and delicate flowers are produced. Each flower has numerous petals, and stamens, and in this respect the bitterroot resembles cacti. The petals are approximately 1 inch long and vary in color from nearly white to deep rose and often have darker longitudinal stripes. The succulent leaves are small (1-3 inches long), club-shaped, and inconspicuous. All are borne at ground level or below from carrot-like roots. The fleshiness of the bitterroot reflects the water storing adaptation which parallels that of cacti and other "desert" succulents. The roots can survive extreme dehydration and because of this ability the name *rediviva* was applied.

In the past, bitterroot was dug by plains Indians and the roots were eaten after having been peeled and boiled. As the plants age the roots become woody and bitter thus the plants were collected early in the spring. This species was also collected by Lewis and Clark along what is now known as the Bitterroot River in Montana. The genus was named in honor of Captain Meriwether Lewis.

The attractive bitterroot—the state flower of Montana — is widely distributed in the sagebrush steppe and along adjacent montane ridges. It flowers in early summer, after most lithosol associates.

Bitterroot

PINK FAMILY (Caryophyllaceae)
Desert sandwort (Arenaria hookeri)—

The desert sandwort is a distinctive plant which forms very dense and tight cushions several inches in diameter. The congested stems are of two types: those which do not bear flowers, are never more than one or two inches tall, and have numerous, opposite, linear and sharp-pointed leaves; and the flowering stems which are somewhat taller, have fewer leaves, and produce several flowers in compact clusters. The flowers are rather showy with sharp-pointed, green-ribbed sepals and somewhat longer, white petals (⅓ inch long).

The generic name is derived from the Latin *arena* which means sand and this characterizes the habitat of the desert sandwort (wort is an old English word for plant).

It is common in sandy or gravelly soil in dry sagebrush plains of the Rocky Mountain Region, mostly east of the Continental Divide. A very similar sand-loving species of Washington, Oregon, and Nevada is **Arenaria franklinii.**

Desert sandwort (A. hookeri)

Desert sandwort (A. franklinii)

43

BUTTERCUP FAMILY (Ranunculaceae)

Sagebrush buttercup (Ranunculus glaberrimus)—Although there are many species of buttercups, most require moist or wet habitats and the generic name is derived in part from the Latin *rana* meaning frog and relating to the aquatic habitat of many or most buttercups. Among those species that are adapted to semi-arid conditions, the sagebrush buttercup is the showiest and probably the most widespread. It is a very early flowering plant that favors the less dry sites and is frequently found growing under large shrubs such as sagebrush or bitterbrush (Purshia tridentata). This buttercup is a small, branched, usually prostrate herb with dark green, rather fleshy, shallowly lobed leaves, and clustered fleshy roots. The flowers usually exceed 1 inch in diameter and have 5 (4-7) very bright, waxy-shiny, yellow petals, smaller yellowish, purplish tinged sepals, and numerous stamens and pistils.

Sagebrush buttercup is found more or less throughout the high plains of the sagebrush steppe and extends into ponderosa pine forests or piñon-juniper woodlands.

Vase flower (Clematis hirsutissima)—Vase flower is a distinctive and attractive plant with its fernlike leaves and unusual flowers. The stems are 12 to 18 inches tall and have several large, extensively-divided leaves. The flowers are solitary, approximately 1 inch long, and nod as inverted vases at the stem tips. As is typical in species of *Clematis,* petals are absent and the sepals are showy. In the vase flower, the sepals are thick and leathery (from which

Sagebrush buttercup

Vase flower

the common name leather flower is derived), and have the unusual color of brownish-purple. Each flower has several woolly ovaries which at maturity have very long, feathery styles. The entire plant is densely hairy.

Vase flower is equally at home in the high plains and in the mountains. It occurs in all but the southernmost part of the steppeland. Some plains Indians considered this plant to have healing powers.

Common larkspur (Delphinium nuttallianum)—Among the many species of larkspur, this is the most variable and widespread. It is distributed from moist mountain meadows and open forests to dry sandy sagebrush plains and, with the exception of some of the drier sites, it occurs essentially throughout the steppe. The variation is expressed in many ways; the normally blue to purple color of the sepals varies to nearly pure white. The roots may be rather thin and woody, thick and fleshy, or intermediate. The upper part of the stem and the flowers are usually hairy, the nature of which varies from sparse to dense and matted or even glandular-sticky.

All larkspurs have bilaterally symmetrical (irregular) flowers with the upper sepal being extended into a rather long, nectar-bearing spur; the two lower petals are much broader and more widely spread than the upper two. The stamens are very numerous and each flower produces three to five pod-like fruits (follicles). The leaves are palmately lobed or divided. The most attractive of the steppe species of larkspur is **Delphinium geyeri,** a blue-flowered plant.

Common larkspur (D. nuttallianum)

Larkspur (D. geyeri)

POPPY FAMILY (Papaveraceae)
Prickly poppy (Argemone platyceras)

—The leaves and stems of the prickly poppy resemble those of thistles but the flowers and fruit are very different. The stems are coarse and branched and are covered by needle-sharp spines and yellow prickles. The leaves are variously lobed, have spines along the margins and midvein, and clasp the stem. The showy flowers are borne on branch tips among the leaves, and each has numerous stamens, three spiny green sepals and six delicate white petals, 2-3 inches long and nearly as wide. The fruit is typical of poppies, with a round base and flattened cap with scalloped edges and small pores through which the seeds are shaken by the wind.

The conspicuous and well marked prickly poppy grows in somewhat sandy and gravelly habitats through much of the southern steppe including southeastern Oregon and a large part of Nevada and adjacent Utah. Like most poppies, it contains isoquinolin (opium-type) alkaloids which are known to be toxic to man and other animals. The plants are rarely eaten, however, either because of their spininess, distastefulness, or both. The seeds probably are eaten by birds and controlled experiments have shown that daily small amounts are fatal to fowl.

Prickly poppy

MUSTARD FAMILY (Cruciferae)

Prince's plume (Stanleya pinnata) — Prince's plume is a rather striking inhabitant of the southern and drier areas of the sagebrush steppe. It is a tall plant (often exceeding 3 feet) with several unbranched stems, each with a terminal, plumelike cluster of small, bright-yellow flowers. The basal leaves are pinnately divided or compound and soon become dry and fall off. The upper, smaller leaves are undivided and more persistent. Like other members of the mustard family, each flower has four sepals and four petals. The fruit is long and narrow.

Prince's plume accumulates selenium from the soil and incorporates it, at the expense of sulfur, into some of its amino acids. The plant tolerates or even benefits by this substitution of selenium for sulfur but animals cannot. To them the chemically and functionally altered amino acids and proteins are highly toxic. Fortunately, the plants are seldom eaten.

Prince's plume is widely distributed in the dry, sandy sagebrush plains and talus slopes of northern Nevada and Utah, southern Idaho and Wyoming, and northeastern Oregon. It also has a broad ecological range extending from the dry, sandy soils of the Mojave Desert to the high, juniper-covered ridges of Colorado.

Thelypodium (Thelypodium laciniatum) —This a rather tall and thick-stemmed, biennial herb with a radishlike taproot. The stems usually have several, strictly erect branches, each terminated by a dense and spirelike cluster (raceme) of flowers and/or fruits. The flowers have four greenish-white

Prince's plume

Thelypodium

47

or occasionally purplish sepals and four narrow, white petals, up to ½ inch long. The fruits are long and narrow and develop from the bottom of the raceme upward. The fleshy leaves are variously toothed and divided and are concentrated near the base of the stems.

Thelypodium is widespread in the deserts and steppes of western North America. It is most frequently found in sandy sagebrush plains and on talus slopes. It flowers in early summer.

Tumbling mustard (Sisymbrium altissimum)—The unattractive tumbling mustard —whose scientific name means very tall, sweet-smelling plant—is a widespread weed of European origin. It occurs chiefly in disturbed areas, particularly those with loose, sandy soil. It is a rather tall (up to 3 feet), much-branched annual with pinnately compound or divided lower leaves and reduced upper ones. The flowers are small and pale yellow and give rise to long, linear, capsulelike fruits. The entire plant has a somewhat circular profile and after death it becomes uprooted and rolls in the wind while spreading its seeds.

This plant should not be confused with the Russian thistle, also a tumbleweed. The tumble mustard is more sparsely branched, has a light straw color, and lacks the spininess of the widespread Russian thistle.

Dagger-pod (Phoenicaulis cheiranthoides) — Dagger-pod is a distinctive plant with a thick, woody rootcrown bearing many narrowly elliptical leaves and several leafless stems. The stems are erect or, more often, spread outward to form a broad ring around the central leaves. The pink to red-

Tumbling mustard

Dagger-pod

48

dish flowers are produced in a congested raceme along the upper (or outer) half of the stem. The fruits mature into daggerlike pods which project outward on short stalks (pedicels), at right angles from the stem. The stem is also often reddish-colored and presumably the generic name relates to this trait (Gr. *phoeni* = reddish-purple, *caulis* = stems). *Cheiranthoides* is translated as a hand of flowers.

Dagger-pod occurs in the high plains and open forests of eastern Washington and Oregon and adjacent Nevada and Idaho. It grows in rocky, thin soils (lithosols) and flowers in early spring.

Bladder-pods (Physaria and Lesquerella species)—The bladder-pods are low mustards with bright yellow flowers. The fruit matures into a round or two-lobed pod

which in many species becomes inflated and bladderlike. Each pod has a single, narrow style.

Both *Lesquerella* and *Physaria* have several weak and spreading stems and numerous leaves, most derived from the woody rootcrown. As is typical for mustards, each flower has four sepals, four petals, and six stamens. An outstanding characteristic of these two groups of bladder-pods is the very dense, star-shaped pubescence (hairs) which cover the stems, leaves, pods, and usually sepals, giving the plants a grayish cast. The subtleties of these hairs can not be appreciated without a microscope.

Species of *Lesquerella* and *Physaria* appear to intergrade and apparently do hybridize when their ranges overlap. Both genera are widely represented in the sagebrush

Bladder-pods (Lesquerella)

steppe and favor gravelly slopes and plains.

Rock cress (Arabis species)—Although the rock cresses are not among the most attractive inhabitants of the sagebrush steppe, they are common, widespread, and are represented by several species. The plants are typified by a combination of characteristics which include upright, usually unbranched stems with a whorl of basal leaves and a few to several "clasping" stem leaves; a linear arrangement of flowers (raceme) along the upper half of the stem; a combination of four sepals, four nonyellow petals, and six stamens; long and narrow fruits which split open at maturity; and branched or star-shaped hairs that can not be observed without a microscope.

Probably the most widespread (and variable) species is **Arabis holboelii** with white or pink flowers and drooping fruits. One of the most attractive species is **A. divaricarpa** with reddish-purple flowers. It occurs in the high plains and mountains.

Western wallflower (Erysimum asperimum) — Western wallflower is one of the most attractive representatives of the large and important mustard family. The numerous showy flowers have four sepals, four bright yellow petals, and six stamens. Each petal has a broad, flat blade and a very narrow base (claw) and is about 1 inch long.

The plants have a single stem which varies in height from 6 to 36 inches. The many narrow and often toothed leaves are most concentrated at the base of the stem. The flowers are produced in a terminal, rather dense cluster (raceme); and the fruits are long and very narrow.

Rock cress (A. divaricarpa)

Western wallflower

CAPER FAMILY (Capparidaceae)

Yellow bee plant (Cleome lutea)—This plant combines a number of features to make it both unusual and very attractive. Most noticeable are its bright, golden-yellow flowers, densely congested into a showy terminal cluster that elongates as the plant matures. Each flower has four narrow sepals, four yellow petals, and six stamens which are considerably longer than the petals and contribute to the general showiness of the flower cluster. The podlike fruits —shaped by the large seeds they contain— develop first at the base of the flower cluster and hang gracefully on narrow stalks (pedicels).

The plants are erect annuals with a single stem which may be as much as 3 feet tall and is often branched. The attractive leaves are palmately compound (lupinelike) with usually five elliptical leaflets. Upper stem leaves are reduced and bractlike.

The yellow bee plant is very common regionally in sandy plains of the western deserts and steppes, and is a conspicuous dominant in some areas of the Great Basin, especially in Utah, and in adjacent Colorado. It flowers over a period of several weeks beginning in late spring.

Yellow bee plant

STONECROP FAMILY (Crassulaceae)

Lance-leaf stonecrop (Sedum lanceolatum)—Stonecrop is an interesting plant with its succulent adaptation to dry and exposed habitats. It often forms rather dense mats, spreading by runners or rootstalks (rhizomes). The stems are of two types, those that produce flowers (about 6 inches tall) and many dwarf stems that appear as bundles of leaves. In the lance-leaf stonecrop, the leaves are nearly round in cross-section, about ½ inch long, and sharp-pointed (lance-shaped). The bright yellow flowers are borne in a rather dense, branched cluster at the stem tips and the five petals of each flower are sharp-pointed and spread to form a star.

The lance-leaf stonecrop has a wide geographical and altitudinal distribution. It ranges from desert to high alpine and from the west coast to the plains of Colorado. Throughout its range it occurs in dry and rocky (lithosol) habitats. It flowers during the summer.

Lance-leaf stonecrop

SAXIFRAGE FAMILY (Saxifragaceae)

Prairie star flower (Lithophragma bulbifera)—There are other species of *Lithophragma* which occur in the steppe, some more showy but none as widespread as the prairie star flower. This is a small reddish-colored herbaceous plant (less than 1 foot tall) with palmately lobed and divided leaves, the well developed ones derived from the base of the plant. The flowers are also small and are borne in an open raceme at the stem tip. The delicate white to pink or purplish petals are deeply divided into several narrow segments. Small reddish bulbs (bulblets) are typically produced in the axil of the reduced stem leaves and among the fibrous roots as well. It has been postulated that these bulblets produce toxins which lead to livestock poisoning when the plants are pulled up by the roots during wet spring weather. However, rodents eat the bulblets without apparent harm.

The prairie star flower extends from dry sagebrush communities to meadows, grassy hillsides, open forests, and rocky ridges. It can be expected in the high plains of all the western states but is rather inconspicuous and flowers very early in the spring.

Prairie star flower

Alumroot (Heuchera cylindrica) — Although the flowers of alumroot are not particularly showy, the plants are attractive in their rocky setting with their numerous dark green, palmately-lobed, basal leaves with long petioles. The stems are leafless, straight, and up to 3 feet tall with a dense terminal spike of cream-colored to greenish-yellow flowers. The petals are small and inconspicuous or absent, and the sepals are fused at the base to form a cup-shaped structure with five lobes. Usually, the plants are covered with short, straight hairs.

This is the most widespread and probably most drought tolerant of several closely related species of *Heuchera*. It occurs on rock ledges and talus slopes in the high plains and mountains of western North America. It is also easily transplanted or grown from seed and makes a desirable contribution to the native rock garden.

Alumroot

SYRINGA FAMILY (Hydrangeace)

Syringa (Philadelphus lewisii)—Syringa is an extensively branched, medium sized shrub which frequents coarse talus slopes and rocky ledges, particularly along canyon walls and dry gullies. It is an extremely attractive shrub with numerous, rather large, very fragrant white flowers. From a distance it is very similar to and often mistaken for serviceberry (Amelanchier), which may occur in similar habitats. Syringa can easily be distinguished, however, by one or a combination of the following characteristics: the leaves and branches are opposite (paired at the nodes); the fruits are woody capsules rather than berries; the leaves are heavily veined and nontoothed; and—most importantly—the flowers have only four rather than five petals. Like serviceberry,

syringa is a preferred deer food.

Syringa ranges from British Columbia through Washington and Oregon and east to Montana. It is widely distributed in northern Idaho of which it is the state flower.

Philadelphus is of Greek derivation *(philos* = love, *delphos* = brother) and the genus was named in honor of Ptolemy II (Philadelphus), who ruled Egypt from 283 to 247 BC. *Philadelphus lewissi* was first collected by Lewis and Clark along the Bitterroot River in Montana and was named in honor of Meriwether Lewis. The common name, syringa, is retained from a time during the middle ages when this genus was combined with lilac in the genus *Syringa.*

Syringa

CURRENT FAMILY (Grossulariaceae)

Squaw currant (Ribes cereum)—Squaw currant is a medium-sized shrub with brownish stems and palmately-lobed, gray-green leaves. The flowers are borne in small clusters along the branches, at the end of short stalks. The sepals are greenish-white to pinkish and are fused into a tube with five spreading lobes. The petals are small, fan-shaped, and inconspicuous. Although the flowers are not particularly showy, the fruit is, becoming orange-red. when ripe. The fruit is not particularly palatable, however, and if eaten in a sufficiently large quantity may result in a burning sensation in the throat. The younger branches, leaf stalks, flowers, and fruits are often sticky with glandular hairs which contribute to the rather strong, unpleasant odor of the plants,

somewhat resembling carrion. Nevertheless, the plants provide an important food source for deer.

Squaw currant is a common shrub on coarse talus slopes — particularly in the higher altitudes and latitudes of the sagebrush steppe—extending upward into open forests and ridges. It is found in suitable habitats more-or-less throughout the steppeland.

Another species of wild currant of occasional occurrence in the steppeland is **golden currant (Ribes aureum),** an attractive shrub with golden-yellow flowers and orangish fruit which is tasty and makes excellent jelly. Its three-lobed leaves are bright green and somewhat leathery. It occurs mainly along the gravel banks and flood plains of streams and rivers.

Squaw currant fruit

Squaw currant

Golden currant

ROSE FAMILY (Rosaceae)

Old man's beard (Geum triflorum) — Although somewhat inconspicuous in its habitat, old man's beard is nevertheless an attractive plant. The basal fernlike leaves are pinnately compound with deeply toothed leaflets that get progressively larger toward the leaf tip. The flowering stems are leafless, with the exception of two, small dissected leaves near midlength. The flowers normally occur in threes (as the species name implies) and are associated with dissected leaflike bracts. The reddish sepals are fused at the base to form a bowl-shaped structure from which the five petals and numerous stamens are derived. The petals are yellow to red and are nearly hidden by the sepals. The entire plant is sparsely to densely covered with long, soft hairs. As the fruits (achenes) mature, the styles become very long and feathery and collectively present the appearance of a long, white beard. The roots have an interesting sassafraslike taste and can be boiled to make a refreshing tea.

This species is widely distributed and occurs in the more moist sites of the steppeland, particularly the high plains of the Rockies, from Canada to Nevada, Arizona, and New Mexico.

Slender cinquefoil (Potentilla gracilis) —*Potentilla* is a complex genus, and slender cinquefoil is the most widespread and variable of the species. It is usually 1-2 feet tall and has several stems and numerous palmately compound leaves, the basal ones having long slender petioles. The common name "cinquefoil" (five-leaf) is not strictly

Old man's beard

Slender cinquefoil

applicable since the leaves have six to nine leaflets, rather than five. The dense foliage is very attractive with deeply toothed leaflets and silky-gray hairiness (pubescence). The showy, bright yellow flowers are produced in a branched, flat-topped cluster (inflorescence) above the leaves. Each flower has five sepals and five lower bracts, five petals, and numerous stamens and small ovaries.

Slender cinquefoil is probably most common in the high plains and mountains where sagebrush communities overlap with open forests. It also extends upward along montane ridges into subalpine meadows and ranges throughout western North America. It flowers in early summer.

Bitterbrush (Purshia tridentata) — Bitterbrush is often a dominant plant in communities immediately below ponderosa pine forests and piñon-juniper woodlands. It is also common on dry, open, south-facing slopes of mountain ridges. In general, it can be expected in somewhat sandy or rocky, well-drained soils in areas somewhat more moist than is typical for the sagebrush steppe. It is usually associated with balsam roots (Balsamorhiza) or dwarf sunflower (Wyethia).

Bitterbrush is a medium-sized, extensively branched shrub with numerous small three-lobed leaves that closely resemble those of sagebrush but lack the gray, woolly hair and are therefore brighter green or sometimes olive-green. The flowers are small but bright yellow and very numerous, giving the shrubs an especially attractive appearance during the flowering period in late spring.

Bitterbrush

Bitterbrush ranges from Washington and Oregon eastward through Wyoming, north into Canada, and south into Utah, Colorado, Nevada, and California. In the southern extreme of its range, it overlaps and hybridizes with the closely related **Cliffrose (Cowania stransburiana).** Although it is a bitter-tasting shrub, it is an extremely important food source for deer, especially in the winter on windswept, relatively snow-free slopes. Here, the plants are often stunted from excessive browsing pressure.

Serviceberry (Amelanchier alnifolia)— Serviceberry is widely distributed over western North America and although it is most common in open forests, it frequently occurs in coarse talus in the sagebrush steppe, particularly along canyon walls. It is also a common inhabitant of aspen groves which themselves exist as "island" communities in the upper sagebrush plains.

Serviceberry is a large, variable-sized shrub with numerous attractive and fragrant white spring flowers which have five rather narrow and elongate petals and numerous stamens. The leaves are ovate to elliptical and are toothed toward the tip. The fruit is bluish-purple when mature and resembles a miniature apple. It is juicy and tasty when eaten fresh and makes good preserves, especially jelly, and pie. It also provides a staple food source for birds and other animals. Serviceberry also has considerable value as a browse plant for wild animals, particularly deer.

Serviceberry

Serviceberry fruit

PEA FAMILY (Leguminosae)

Locoweed (Astragalus species)—Within the sagebrush steppe, no other genus has as many species as *Astragalus,* many very similar and difficult to distinguish. Still, within the genus as a whole there is considerable variation. Most species are low spreading plants but some may be more than 2 feet tall. The flowers, although all generally pealike, vary considerably in size and color. As is true of all legumes, the fruit is a pod, but there is little uniformity in its nature and size. Most plants have pinnately compound leaves, but the size and shape of the leaflets of different species is inconsistent. Finally, there is a wide range of ecological adaptations shown by the numerous species. However, most occur in rather dry, open areas and the steppeland appears to provide ideal habitats for many. This is especially true in and around Wyoming where locoweeds are most prevalent.

Locoweeds represent a dual threat in terms of livestock poisoning. Several species have the ability to accumulate large amounts of selenium which upsets the protein metabolism of animals which feed on the plants. This causes acute poisoning and often death. In addition, many or most species contain an alkaloidlike substance, "locine". The effects of locine are cumulative and large amounts of the plants must be eaten often over a period of several days before the symptoms begin to occur. Normally animals avoid locoweed unless food is scarce, but many get "hooked" or develop the "loco habit." The disease gets its name from the associated symptoms of

Near Wenatchee, Washington

lack of coordination and muscular control coupled with violent and unpredictable behavior when aroused. Animals rarely recover completely after having suffered from loco poisoning.

Three of the many important species of *Astragalus* are **A. bisulcatus**—a tall, many-stemmed plant with elongate clusters (racemes) of white or violet flowers, a plant which is very common and conspicuous in the sagebrush plains of the Rocky Mountain region; **A. purshii**—a low and dense cushion plant with colorful, usually reddish-purple flowers and white-woolly pods, a plant occurring throughout the sagebrush steppe in rocky, thin soils (lithosols); **A. miser**—a highly variable, low plant with short clusters (racemes) of white and purplish flowers and narrow, straight pods, a

plant occurring more or less throughout the steppe. A common sand-loving species of Washington and Oregon is **A. succumbens.** A species easily recognized by its grape-like fruits is **A. crassicarpus.**

A closely related genus of similar distribution is *Oxytropis* which can usually be distinguished by its lack of stem leaves, the leaves all being derived from the rootcrown. Species of this genus have poisonous properties similar to *Astragalus* and are also called locoweed. The two most widespread species are **Oxytropis sericeus (silver locoweed)** and **O. lambertii (Rocky Mountain locoweed),** both common in the high plains of the eastern steppe (Great Basin area) extending westward into Idaho. Both have white or violet flowers and silky gray pubescence (hairiness).

Locoweed (A. bisulcatus)

Locoweed (A. miser)

Locoweed (A. purshii)

Locoweed (A. succumbens)

Sweetvetch (Hedysarum boreale)—This species, also called Northern Hedysarum, closely resembles some of the larger loco-weeds *(Astragalus species)* and occurs in similar habitats. It differs, however, in having more attractive, red or purplish-red flowers and flattened pods with obvious constrictions between the seeds. The plants are "bushy" in having many branched stems, 1-2 feet tall. The leaves are pinnately compound with 7-15 oval leaflets. The reddish flowers are irregular (bilaterally symmetrical) and pealike and are congested into elongate, showy racemes. The generic name is of Greek derivation (*hedy* = sweet, *sarum* = broom) and probably relates to the pleasant fragrance of the flowers and broomlike aspect of the erect, many-stemmed plants.

Sweetvetch ranges from the arctic tundra in Canada into the southern Rockies. It is fairly common in the high plains, especially in the Rocky Mountain region, where it grows in fine textured, often clayey soils. It flowers in early summer or late spring.

Unlike locoweed, sweetvetch is not poisonous and, in fact, has a history of having been collected and eaten by Indians. The roots especially are tasty (licoricelike) and nutritious.

Lupine (Lupinus species)—Some of the most frequent associates of sagebrush are the various species of lupine, often difficult to distinguish from each other but clearly distinct from other genera. The most outstanding characteristic of lupines is the palmately-compound leaves with 4-8 elongate leaflets all derived from the same point on

Locoweed (A. crassicarpus)

Silver locoweed

Sweetvetch

Sweetvetch

63

the petiole. Lupine flowers are pealike, usually blue and white or occasionally yellowish, and are borne in rather dense, headlike or, more frequently, elongate clusters (racemes) at the tip of hollow stems or branches. Most plants are densely hairy, a water-retaining adaptation.

Like other legumes, lupines fix nitrogen thus making a significant ecological contribution to the steppe, particularly to nitrogen deficient sandy soils. They are also important in a negative way because they contain poisonous alkaloids. Livestock poisoning frequently occurs when hungry animals, particularly sheep, are trailed through lupine populations feeding on the toxic seeds and podlike fruits.

Of the several steppe species of lupine, only a few of the most prevalent are discussed here.

Dry-ground lupine (Lupinus aridus) is a distinctive, compact, cushionlike plant of dry, rocky, thin soils (lithosols). The flowers are blue (or violet) and white (rarely totally white) and are borne in dense elliptical clusters that are partially hidden by the leaves. This is an early flowering lupine of Washington, Oregon and Idaho, ranging south into Nevada and California.

Silky lupine (L. sericeus) is a tall, branched plant with few to several elongate clusters (racemes) of blue to lavender flowers. The narrow leaflets are densely white-hairy (silky) on both surfaces. This species is widespread and common in the dry sagebrush plains of North America.

Plains lupine (L. wyethii) is a medium-sized, non-branched plant with long, spire-

Dry-ground lupine

Plains lupine

Velvet lupine

shaped flower clusters and violet (or purple) and white flowers. It is most common in the high plains of the Rocky Mountains.

Velvet lupine (L. leucophyllus) is a coarse, tall unbranched lupine with a long, congested, spikelike cluster of lavender to white flowers. This densely-hairy plant is widespread but of sporadic occurrence in the high plains of the sagebrush steppe.

Sulphur lupine (L. sulphureus) is one of a few lupines with pale yellowish flowers. It is a medium-sized, branched plant which occurs in gravelly soils in the plains of Washington, Oregon, and California.

Foothills lupine (L. ammophilus) is one of the most attractive lupines of the steppe, with its showy racemes of blue-violet and white flowers. It occurs in the high plains of Utah and Colorado.

Three additional lupines of wide distribution and high frequency of occurrence in the steppeland are **silvery lupine (L. argenteus), tailcup lupine (L. caudatus),** and **Great Basin lupine (L. greenei).** All are blue- to violet-flowered, rather tall species.

Golden pea (Thermopsis montana)— The showy, golden-yellow flowers and the graceful three-foliate leaves — with basal leafy stipules—combine to make the golden pea a very attractive plant. The stems are coarse, up to nearly 3 feet tall, and bear several leaves. The flowers are pealike and are borne in a somewhat elongate but usually dense cluster (raceme). The sepals and the upper part of the stem are usually silky-hairy as are the narrow, erect pods.

The golden pea rather closely resembles

Sulphur lupine

Golden pea

Foothills lupine

lupine in many respects and the name *Thermopsis* is derived from the Greek *thermos* meaning lupine and *opsis* which means resemblance. However, none of the lupines has such bright yellow flowers and all have more than three leaflets.

The golden pea occurs most frequently in meadows where it often forms dense populations, partly as a result of its unpalatability. Occasionally it can be found in the moister areas of the high plains. It is widespread in western North America, from the west coast into Colorado.

Large-headed clover (Trifolium macrocephalum)—This species is unusual in a number of respects. While most clovers grow in moist soils or as weeds in disturbed areas, the large-headed clover is certainly not weedy and grows only in thin, rocky (lithosol) areas which become very dry during the hot summer months. Clovers, of course, are characterized by having three (tri) leaflets (folium) but the large-headed clover has five or six and in this respect the leaves resemble those of lupines.

The large-headed clover is also our most attractive species of *Trifolium*. It is a sprawling, hairy plant that spreads by rootstalks (rhizomes) and forms extensive populations. The pink to lavender, pealike flowers are densely congested into showy heads 1½ to 2 inches in diameter.

This clover is a regular member of lithosol communities in eastern Washington and adjacent Oregon and Idaho. It extends southward into Nevada and upward into similar habitats in ponderosa pine forests. It flowers in the springtime.

Large-headed clover

GERANIUM FAMILY (Geraniaceae)

Wild geranium (Geranium viscosissi-mum) — Of the several species of wild geranium, this is the most attractive and most widespread. It is about 2 feet tall, has many leafy stems, and is more or less covered by glandular-sticky hairs. The glandular exudation is responsible for the typical geranium odor and the species' name. The leaves are palmately divided into sharply toothed segments. The flowers are saucer-shaped with five pink to lavender-purple or sometimes white petals, each somewhat less than ½ inch long. The fruit is a long "beaked" structure which splits from the base into five one-seeded segments. The long beak is responsible for a second common name for the genus, crane's bill. In fact, the name geranium is derived from the Greek *geranos* meaning crane.

This wild geranium is most frequent in and around the upper limits of the sagebrush steppe and is common in aspen groves. It occurs in suitable habitats throughout western North America. It is a favorite forage plant for several animals, especially elk and moose both of which prefer the flowers.

Wild geranium

FLAX FAMILY (Linaceae)

Wild flax (Linum perenne)—Flax is well marked and easily distinguished from all other inhabitants of the sagebrush steppe. It is a rather tall plant (up to 3 feet) with several unbranched stems derived from a somewhat woody rootcrown. The leaves are numerous, narrow, and average approximately 1 inch in length. The most conspicuous aspect of flax is its showy sky-blue flowers (1-2 inches across) borne near the tip of the thin, flexuous stems. The attractive petals, five per flower, soon fall off if the stems are broken; therefore the flowers cannot be picked for bouquets.

Flax is an extremely widely distributed plant, occurring in suitable habitats throughout the sagebrush steppe. Most frequently it is found in sandy plains where it is commonly associated with sagebrush or rabbitbrush *(Chrysothamnus)*. However, it may extend well up into the mountains where it grows on non-forested gravelly ridges—again associated with sagebrush—or in open Savannalike forests such as piñon-juniper woodlands or ponderosa pine communities.

Like the cultivated form, flax has tough fibrous stems which can be used for making cordage. Indians used flax twine in many ways, including fishing lines and net construction.

Wild flax

MALLOW FAMILY (Malvaceae)

Orange globe mallow (Sphaeralcea munroana) — Because of the unusual orange coloration of its flowers, orange globe mallow is a conspicuous and easily recognized species. The five colorful petals are approximately ½ inch long and overlap somewhat, collectively forming an attractive bowl-shaped structure. The stamens are very numerous and are fused together at their base forming a tube around the lower part of the style. The leaves are dark green to somewhat grayish—due to a dense covering of minute, star-shaped hairs—and are palmately lobed resembling those of geraniums. The plants are widely branched with a strong woody root system that penetrates to great depths below the earth surface.

The orange globe mallow is an extremely adaptable and widely distributed species. It can be found in many different soil types but "prefers" moderately sandy or rocky sites. It occurs throughout the ecological extreme of the sagebrush steppe and extends southward into the drier Sonoran and Mojave Deserts. In the eastern steppe (Great Basin area) this species is replaced by the similar **scarlet globe mallow (Sphaeralcea coccinea)** which has somewhat redder (to scarlet) flowers and more deeply divided leaves.

The generic name is of Greek derivation, *spaera* means globelike and refers to the round fruit with pie-shaped segments; *alcea* means mallow: globe mallow.

Orange globe mallow

Scarlet globe mallow

VIOLET FAMILY (Violaceae)

Sagebrush violet (Viola trinervata) — Violets and pansies are associated typically with cool, moist habitats of forests and meadows. However, sagebrush violet is exceptional in that it grows only in poorly developed soils of rock formations. Here, the fleshy roots penetrate in small crevices to moderate depths and absorb the spring moisture that collects. Flowering occurs very early in the spring and by summer the dormant plants have become dried up and appear dead.

The flowers of sagebrush violet are very showy and closely resemble those of cultivated pansies although somewhat smaller. The two upper petals are reddish-violet; the three lower ones are lilac-colored with purple lines and a yellowish base. The leaves are rather distinctive, being somewhat fleshy and leathery and being divided into a number of strongly veined leaflets or leaf segments. This species is rather common in lithosol communities of central Washington and northern Oregon.

Sagebrush violet

LOASA FAMILY (Loasaceae)
Blazing star (Mentzelia laeviculmis)—

Blazing star injects great beauty into the usually drab setting of the mid or late summer steppeland. Its brilliant, lemon-yellow flowers are large and showy with five or more widely spreading, sharp-pointed petals which collectively form a nearly perfect star. The stamens are also yellow, are very numerous, and are projected forward from the center of the "star," providing it with a blazing appearance. The sepals are very narrow, somewhat shorter than and alternate with the 2 inch petals. With age the sepals become twisted and leathery, remaining as appendages on the mature, somewhat woody capsular fruit. The whitish stems are branched with alternate, deeply lobed leaves. Both the stems and the leaves are covered with very harsh, sticky, sandpaperlike pubescence.

Blazing star is a short-lived, occasional plant on fine talus slopes and gravelly sagebrush plains. It is particularly conspicuous because of its attractiveness and its distribution along cut-banks and gravel shoulders of highways.

Blazing star

71

CACTUS FAMILY (Cactaceae)

Prickly pear cactus (Opuntia poly-acantha)—Few plants have flowers as attractive as cacti in general and prickly pear in particular. In this species the flowers are usually lemon-yellow or peach-color (becoming pink or orange with age) but may be brilliant red as they frequently are in Nevada and southern Idaho. The multi-petaled flowers are produced as outgrowths from terminal, somewhat flattened, pear-shaped stem segments which are well armed with long, needle-sharp spines. *(Polyacantha* means many spines.)

Like other species of cacti, the prickly pear has a much-branched shallow root system which enables the plants to absorb water rapidly after rainstorms. Also as in other cacti, water is stored in the succulent stems and is used during periods of drought.

Prickly pear is widespread and variable in habit. It occurs most frequently in sandy soils where individual plants tend to be rather widely scattered. However, over-grazing leads to an increased density as a result of the elimination of competitors, the creation of new, disturbed habitats, and the physical dissemination of stem segments each of which has the ability to develop into a new plant.

Hedgehog cactus (Pediocactus simp-sonii)—The hedgehog cactus is somewhat of an oddity in the sagebrush steppe and would seem to be more at home in the succulent deserts of the southwest, together with the numerous other round or barrel-shaped cacti of that region. It is a small cactus, seldom over 6 inches tall, and often

Prickly pear cactus

Prickly pear cactus

Prickly pear cactus

72

occurs in small clumps. The round stems are covered with vertical rows of tubercles (swollen areas) each of which has several spreading, rigid, needle-sharp spines. The showy rose to purple or yellowish flowers are borne without stalks at the top of the cactus. Each flower is 1 to 1½ inches wide and has numerous petals and stamens.

Hedgehog cactus is much less common than the prickly pear and tends to be restricted to rocky hillsides and plains, usually in lithosol areas. It does have a wide range, however, including the large part of the sagebrush steppe.

Hedgehog cactus

EVENING PRIMROSE FAMILY
(Onagraceae)

Clarkia (Clarkia pulchella)—The flowers of this species are highly attractive with their distinctive pink-lavender to rose-purple, or rarely white, petals which are approximately 1 inch long with a broad, three-lobed tip and a very narrow minutely toothed base. All floral parts occur in sets of four: four petals, four sepals (all fused together on one side of the flower), four functional and four nonfunctional stamens, four chambers in the ovary, and an elongate conspicuous four-lobed style. As in other members of the evening primrose family (Onagraceae), the ovary is inferior (below the floral parts) and develops into an elongate many-seeded capsule which splits open at maturity.

Clarkia is a locally common, widely-distributed annual. It occurs in dry, sandy open areas in forested regions or in similar habitats in the steppeland where it is associated with sagebrush. This genus was named in honor of Captain William Clark of the Lewis and Clark Expedition. The species name, *pulchella,* means beautiful and is appropriately applied to this plant.

Evening primrose (Oenothera species) —This genus comprises a number of attractive, fragrant and often nocturnal desert and/or steppe species. As a group they are recognizable by a combination of four petals, eight stamens, and a long, narrow floral tube arising from the ovary which matures into an oblong or elliptical, often coiled capsule. Most species are low, essentially stemless plants with many basal leaves.

Clarkia

Clarkia

74

The most widespread and attractive evening primrose is **Desert Evening primrose (Oenothera caespitosa)** with its large and showy white flowers that turn pink with age, both colors frequently occurring on the same plant. The petals are as much as 2 inches long and wide, and are deeply notched at the tip (heart-shaped). The plants lack stems thus the flowers and elongate, toothed leaves are borne on the rootcrown. This species occurs most requently on talus slopes or in sandy plains and is widely distributed in western North America.

A very similar but short-stemmed, somewhat smaller-flowered species is **hairy evening primrose (O. deltoides).** This plant has a more southerly distribution occurring more frequently in the Mojave Desert than in the sagebrush steppe.

White-stemmed evening primrose (O. pallida) is a common species of partially stabilized sand dunes and other sandy areas on the west side of the Continental Divide. It has stems up to 18 inches tall with many narrow and elongate, often toothed leaves. The flowers are borne in the axils of the upper leaves and are white or pink with age. The petals are approximately 1 inch long.

A species from east of the Continental Divide that somewhat resembles the white-stemmed evening primrose in form and size is **O. trichocalyx.** This species is widespread on gravelly hillsides and in sandy plains of Wyoming, Colorado, and Utah.

Two attractive yellow-flowered evening primroses are tansy-leaved evening primrose **(O. tanecetifolia)** and **O. brachy-**

Desert evening primrose

White-stemmed evening primrose

Evening primrose (O. brachycarpa)

75

carpa. The latter is a large-flowered, stemless species of southerly distribution, reaching the sagebrush steppe in Nevada. It has bright yellow petals which turn reddish with age. Oenothera tanecetifolia occurs in lowland, moist areas—with heavy loam or clay soils—on the west side of the Continental Divide. It is a low, stemless plant with deeply lobed or divided leaves and brilliant yellow flowers. The petals are somewhat less than 1 inch long.

Tansy-leaved evening primrose

PARSLEY FAMILY (Umbelliferae)

Desert parsley (Lomatium species) — Several species of *Lomatium* occur in the sabebrush steppe, many of which are extremely common. All have divided, fernlike or carrotlike leaves (although in some species the leaf segments are rather large), and all have very small flowers which are crowded into one or more umbrellalike clusters (umbels). In most species the flowers are yellow, but in **salt & pepper (L. gormanii),** a very early flowering plant, the flowers are white with contrasting dark anthers. In **L. dissectum,** a very robust species, the flowers are often deep purple to almost black. Three of the most common yellow flowered species are: **L. grayi,** with carrotlike leaves; **L. triternatum,** with narrow and elongate (up to 4 inches) leaf seg-

ments; and **L. nudicaule,** with toothed, oval leaf segments which are usually more than an inch long and nearly as wide. All species have somewhat flattened and usually winged seeds that somewhat resemble those of sunflowers. The derivation of the generic name is from the Greek *loma* which means wing or border and refers to the fruit.

Many species have fleshy tuberous or bulblike roots which can be beaten or ground into "flour" from which breadlike foods can be prepared. From this use, the genus or certain species have come to be known as "biscuitroot." These plants provided an important food source for plains Indians and many people continue to collect and eat the plants today.

Although somewhat diverse in habitat, species of desert parsley usually occur in

Desert parsley (L. gormanii)

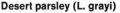

Desert parsley (L. grayi)

Desert parsley (L. dissectum)

Desert parsley (L. triternatum)

somewhat sandy soil in association with sagebrush. Most species occur in the higher or northern, more moist plains, but species can be found throughout the sagebrush steppe.

Yampah (Perideridia species)—Yampah is a delicate and attractive plant. Its leaves are divided with long and very narrow (linear) segments. Its minute, white flowers are borne in dense, ball-like clusters, several of which form an umbrellalike inflorescence. The entire plant has a somewhat lacy appearance.

Yampah was named by plains Indians who collected the plants for their elongate, starchy bulbs, usually two per plant. The bulbs were and are eaten fresh, cooked, dried and stored, or ground into a flour and used for baking. In any case, this is one of the most nourishing and savory wild plants. The generic name is derived from the Greek *perideri* which means necklace. How the name relates to this plant is uncertain.

Yampah often forms extensive populations in high moist plains and sagebrush slopes in the mountains. Frequently it can be found in open conifer or aspen forests, ranging upward to subalpine meadows. It flowers throughout the summer months, the leaves drying up and falling off late in the season.

Yampah

PRIMROSE FAMILY (Primulaceae)

Shooting star (Dodecatheon pauciflorum)

— Although the shooting star is a moisture loving plant and therefore occurs most frequently in meadows and somewhat marshy sites, it is neverthless an occasional inhabitant of sagebrush communities in the high plains and foothills. Here it grows in ravines and other areas where the runoff from melting snow maintains a high level of soil moisture until well into the growing season. It completes its reproductive cycle very quickly during the moist period.

The attractive shooting star is easily identified by its elongate, somewhat strap-like leaves (all basal) and, especially its characteristic and unusual floral structure consisting of five sepals and five petals reflexed backward away from the colorful stamens which are more or less fused into a tube surrounding the style. The total effect of the nodding, purplish-lavender (or white) flower is that of an object speeding toward earth. Even in the days of Greek mythology this genus was respected for its beauty and/or unusual appearance as attested to by its name *dodeca* (twelve) *theon* (gods). The twelve gods assumed the responsibility of watching over some member or members of this genus.

Shooting star

PHLOX FAMILY (Polemoniaceae)

Large-flowered collomia (Collomia grandiflora) — Although this is not one of the most conspicuous species of the steppe, it does have very attractive flowers with an unusual pale-salmon color. The plant is a tall annual (up to three feet) with a single stem which is often branched along the upper half. The leaves are 2-4 inches long, lance-shaped or elliptical, and borne uniformly along the stem. The flowers are produced over an extended period in a showy round-topped head. Each flower has five sepals and five petals, the latter fused into a long and very narrow, nectar-containing tube with perpendicular lobes. Stamens are dark-colored and occur near the "throat" of the floral tube.

The large-flowered collomia occurs sporadically in dry, sandy habitats over a broad geographical range west of the Continental Divide. It flowers in late spring.

A much smaller, related plant is **narrow-leafed collomia (Collomia linearis),** an extremely common but rather inconspicuous annual. Its stems are variable in height, depending on soil conditions, but are rarely more than 1 foot tall. The leaves are narrowly lance-shaped and are borne along the full length of the stem. The petals are fused into a very narrow tube with five short spreading lobes, and vary in color from the usual pink to pale blue or white. The few to several flowers are produced in a condensed head at the tip of the leafy stem.

The narrow-leafed collomia is an early flowering plant of high plains and open mountain ridges and often occurs in associ-

Large-flowered collomia

Narrow-leafed collomia

ation with sagebrush. It can be found in suitable habitats throughout western North America.

Phlox (Phlox species)—Phlox is a Greek word meaning flame and is a fitting name for this group of plants with their condensed mass of brilliant color. The predominant flower color is pink but may vary to blue or lilac-purple or, not infrequently, to white. The plants are usually extensively branched, are often low and cushionlike, and are somewhat shrubby at the base. The leaves are numerous, opposite at the condensed nodes, narrow, and often sharp-pointed. The petals are fused to form a trumpet-shaped structure with a long, narrow tube and five flaring lobes. Neither the stamens nor the style extends beyond the floral tube.

Among the several species of phlox, **P. longifolia** is the most common and widespread, occurring more or less throughout the high plains of the sagebrush steppe. It is a rather weak-stemmed pink-flowered plant that is frequently found extending upward through and clambering over the branches of sagebrush. A similar species, **P. speciosa,** is somewhat more restricted in distribution, being absent in the southern and eastern part of the sagebrush steppe, and is distinguished by its heart-shaped petal lobes. Also, it sometimes has white flowers.

A very common low, compact cushion plant is **P. hoodii** which is found throughout the sagebrush steppe, mostly in dry, rocky (lithosol) habitats. Its showy flowers vary in color from purple to shades of blue, red, or occasionally white. A less compact, mostly

Phlox (P. longifolia)

Phlox (P. hoodii)

Phlox (P. speciosa)

Phlox (P. multiflora)

white-flowered species is **P. multiflora** which is widespread in the high plains and along dry rocky ridges of the Rocky Mountain region.

As a group, the phloxes are among the most desirable wildflower rock garden plants, combining beauty with ease of growth in dry climates.

Granite gilia (Leptodactylon pungens) —If the flowering plants of the steppe were given points for desirable characteristics such as attractiveness of the flowers, and lost points for undesirable properties, granite gilia may well end up with a negative value—unless the "judge" was kind. It is a low spreading shrub with numerous small, spine-tipped leaves that are clustered at the nodes. (Gr. *Lepto* = fine, *dactylo* = finger; Latin *pungens* = spinelike.) Dead leaves

often remain on the branches becoming unsightly and rigidly spiny. The white to salmon-colored flowers are not unattractive but are seldom observed fully open. At night they open and are pollinated by nocturnal moths. During the day they close or partially close in a twisting pattern. The flowers have a long, narrow tube with five spreading petal lobes, and are loosely clustered near the ends of the leafy branches.

Granite gilia is widely distributed in the steppes and deserts of North America, usually occurring in rocky, lithosol areas and on coarse talus (or granitic) slopes.

Scarlet gilia (Gilia aggregata)—Scarlet gilia is a conspicuous plant with strikingly attractive, trumpet-shaped flowers which vary in color from typically brilliant scarlet — speckled with white — to pale pink (or

Granite gilia

Scarlet gilia

82

yellowish) speckled with red. The lighter colored forms are more common in Nevada, Utah, and southern Wyoming. The typical form is distributed throughout the sagebrush steppe, extending upward into piñon-juniper woodlands and open ponderosa pine forests, and onto mountain ridges.

Stems of the scarlet gilia are up to 3 feet tall and often branched, have several flowers, and are derived from an elongate, carrotlike taproot. Most of the attractively lobed and divided leaves are borne at the base of the stem. Often the stems and leaves are glandular-sticky and fragrant.

Scarlet gilia is a biennial. The first year each plant consists of a clump of divided leaves that produce an abundance of food which is stored in the enlarged taproot. The second year the plant uses the stored food to grow and reproduce very rapidly after which time it dies.

Scarlet gilia

WATERLEAF FAMILY (Hydrophyllaceae)

Dwarf waterleaf (Hydrophyllum capitatum)—Dwarf waterleaf is an unusual but very attractive plant. It tends not to be readily noticeable, however, because it usually occurs in thickets or beneath associated shrubs, such as sagebrush, and because the flowers are rather dark colored in a dull, shady background. The blue-purple to lavender flowers are densely congested into a ball-shaped cluster (inflorescence) borne near the base of the plant. The stamens extend well beyond the sepals and petals giving the inflorescence a bristly appearance. The leaves are pinnately compound and the leaflets are variously lobed. The stems and leaf stalks (petioles) are somewhat soft and fleshy but there seems to be little justification for the name, Hydrophyllum (Gr. hydro = water, phyllum = leaf) unless it relates to the fact that water tends to be collected and held by the leaves.

Dwarf waterleaf extends over a broad altitudinal range, from the high plains to subalpine meadows. It is most often found along the border between lower forest or woodland habitats and the sagebrush steppeland. It occurs in sites of sufficient spring moisture throughout the limits of the sagebrush steppe and flowers very early in the spring.

White-leafed phacelia (Phacelia hastata)—White-leafed phacelia is the most variable and one of the least attractive of several species in the genus Phacelia. It gets its name from the silky-white pubescence (hairiness) of the leaves. The variation of the plants is expressed in terms of

Dwarf waterleaf

White-leafed phacelia

size (from a few inches to 3 feet) and flower color, from typically whitish to shades of blue in montane forms. The leaves are narrowly elliptical and many have a pair of lobes at the base of the blade. The upper leaves are reduced in size. The flowers are congested into a number of coiled clusters that appear bristly as a result of the long stamens which extend beyond the fused, funnel-shaped petals with five lobes.

White-leafed phacelia occurs in the high plains and on mountain ridges throughout western North America. It is found most frequently in sandy or gravelly sites and flowers in early summer.

Narrow-leafed phacelia (Phacelia linearis)—In moist years the narrow-leafed phacelia is a common and beautiful plant. The stems are up to 18 inches tall and are often branched, bearing several pale lavender to dark blue showy flowers. In dry years, or in especially dry habitats, the plants are small, unbranched and have only one or a few pale-colored flowers. In either case the leaves are narrow, elongate and sometimes have two basal lobes; the sepals are narrow and hairy; and the five petals are fused at the base to form a cup-shaped structure with projected stamens.

Narrow-leafed phacelia is an annual plant which is widespread in the dry plains and foothills of western North America. It is found most frequently in sandy soils where it often forms rather dense populations. It flowers in the springtime.

Golden gilia **(Phacelia adenophora)**— The golden gilia is a beautiful annual with its many bright, golden-yellow or lavender

Narrow-leafed phacelia

Golden gilia

tinged flowers which tend to be grouped near the ends of low spreading branches. The attractive leaves are pinnately divided and are concentrated near the base of the near-prostrate, branched stem. The petals are approximately ¼ inch long and are fused at the base forming a saucer with 5 lobes. The 5 stamens and the base of the "saucer" are hairy.

The golden gilia is found in the sagebrush zone of northeastern California and adjacent Oregon and Nevada. It occurs in slightly alkaline areas where it frequently forms very dense and showy populations. It flowers in late May and early June.

Hesperochiron (Hesperochiron pumilus)—Although this species has apparently never been given a common name, it well might be called "false strawberry"

since it superficially resembles the wild strawberry. It is a low, spreading plant with white strawberrylike flowers. It has only five (rather than numerous) stamens, however, and the petals are fused at their base into a short, hairy-throated tube. The leaves are also clearly distinct from those of strawberries, being non-lobed, fleshy, and elliptical.

This and other species of *Hesperochiron* occur in swales or other moist sites more or less throughout the sagebrush steppe. Although fairly common, they are infrequently observed since the flowering time, in early spring, is of short duration and the plants are often rather well hidden by larger plants, such as sagebrush.

Hesperochiron

BORAGE FAMILY (Boraginaceae)

Blue bell (Mertensia longiflora)—The beautiful, early-flowering blue bell is fairly common in areas of abundant spring moisture in the high plains of the steppe and in open coniferous forests. It is rather succulent and has branched tuberous roots, 6-8 inch stems, and leathery, bluish leaves which are broadest toward the tip. Each plant has one to several leafy stems with congested nodding or drooping flowers. The petals are fused into a tube with an expanded, lobed tip and they separate very easily from the rest of the flower. The nodding characteristic and tubular petals give the flowers a bell-like appearance. The floral color is sky blue or darker, often fading to pinkish with age.

Blue bells occur most frequently beneath sagebrush "canopies" and in other sheltered sites in the western "half" of the steppeland.

Puccoon (Lithospermum ruderale) — This plant is a rather unattractive herb with a large cluster of leafy stems derived from a strong woody root. The narrow leaves are 1-4 inches long, the lower ones further reduced in size. The flowers are pale (dull) yellow or greenish and are intermixed with and partially hidden by the numerous leaves near the stem tip. The petals are fused at the base into a narrow tube with five spreading lobes resembling a star. Each flower produces four cone-shaped, hard and bony seeds (Gr. *litho* = stone, *sperm* = seed).

Puccoon has a wide range in western North America, occurring in a number of habitats from sandy plains and gravelly

Blue bell

Puccoon

slopes to deep loamy soils of grasslands. It flowers in late spring.

This and a related species are two of many plants which were widely used by plains Indians as a medicine. The roots had a dual function, both as a food (when cooked) and a remedy for certain ailments. The common name is of Indian derivation.

Fiddle-neck (Amsinckia species)—Species of *Amsinckia* are distinguishable from other plants of the steppeland by a *combination* of three conspicuous characteristics: yellow flowers, coarsely hairy stems and leaves, and coiled (scorpioid) flower clusters. All of several species are annuals with a simple taproot and a branched stem. The leaves are rather narrow and elongate, much longer toward the base of the stem. The petals are fused into a nar-row tube with five perpendicularly spreading lobes and are nearly hidden by dense hairs which characteristically occur throughout the plant. These hairs are stiff and bristlelike, sometimes penetrating the skin on contact and then often causing irritation. Each flower produces four small, hard-shelled, black and shiny nutlets which are reputed to be poisonous to cattle.

Fiddle-neck species are difficult to distinguish. They have similar characteristics and all are weedy plants which thrive on disturbed areas such as roadsides and overgrazed ranges; they cannot compete successfully in unaltered plant communities. Various species occur more or less throughout the sagebrush steppe and flower during the springtime.

Cryptanth (Cryptantha species)—*Cryp-*

Fiddle-neck

tantha is a rather large genus with several species occurring in the sagebrush steppe, including annual, biennial, and perennial herbs. Most are small (less than 18 inches tall), coarsely hairy or bristly plants with rather inconspicuous flowers. The small petals are white or rarely yellow and are fused into a tube with five spreading lobes. Often, they are more-or-less hidden by bristly-hairy sepals. The most attractive species are erect perennials with congested flower clusters (inflorescences) and many basal, non-lobed leaves.

Two of the showiest white-flowered species are **Cryptantha glomerata**—a common plant of sandy and gravelly sites in Wyoming, Utah, and Colorado; and **C. leucophylla** — a sand-loving species of eastern Washington and ·adjacent Oregon.

The most attractive of all cryptanths is **C. flava,** a bright yellow-flowered plant occurring frequently in sandy plains of the Great Basin.

Cryptanth (C. glomerata)

Cryptanth (C. flava)

MINT FAMILY (Labiatae)

Purple sage (Salvia dorrii) — Purple sage is a conspicuous low to medium-sized shrub which is easily recognized by its very strong minty-sage odor and elegant and fragrant blue-violet flowers. It is a symmetrical, extensively branched plant with numerous narrow, thickened, opposite leaves. Flowers are borne in whorls at the ends of upright branches and are associated with thickened purplish bracts. The petals are elaborately designed for insect pollination with a basal, nectar-containing tube, a broad, lobed lower lip or landing platform, two lateral lobes and two upright lobes. The two stamens and style are positioned to brush the insects' (bees') back.

Purple sage is found most frequently on partially stabilized talus slopes, rock outcrops, or rocky plains, and is often a dominant member of the community in which it occurs. It is irregularly distributed from eastern Washington and Oregon south and east through southern Idaho and Nevada to Utah.

Purple sage

90

Purple sage

FIGWORT FAMILY (Scrophulariaceae)

Penstemon or beardtongue (Penstemon species) — The various species of penstemon include some of the most beautiful plants of the sagebrush steppe. The flowers are both colorful and attractively structured. The color varies from white to yellowish or pale lavender to, most frequently, deep blue or purple. The petals are fused into a nectar-containing tube with five lobes, two projected upward, the other three usually extended downward and outward providing a landing platform for nectar-seeking bees. Penstemons — especially red-flowered species—which lack the well differentiated landing platforms are adapted for pollination by hummingbirds. The throat of the floral tube is often covered with short hairs which collect pollen and may add to the attractiveness of the flower.

The penstemon flower has five stamens (penta-stamen), only four of which are functional (fertile, or pollen-producing). The fifth, sterile stamen has become variously modified in the process of evolution. Frequently it is covered with golden hair, and within the throat of the floral tube it gives the fancied appearance of a bearded tongue, hence the frequently used common name of beard-tongue.

Penstemon plants usually have several rather coarse, erect stems with opposite (paired), sometimes toothed or lobed leaves. The basal leaves are usually elliptical and have petioles (stalks); the upper leaves lack petioles and are often lance-shaped. The flowers are borne in whorls of a few to several in the axils of the upper

Showy penstemon

92

leaves which progressively become smaller and more bractlike toward the stem tip. The fruit is a hard, somewhat woody capsule which splits open at maturity releasing the numerous small seeds.

Most of the many species of penstemon occur in moderately dry, somewhat sandy soils or on rocky ridges in the mountains. Other species are inhabitants of lithosol, talus, or sandy zones.

One of the most widespread, largest, and most attractive penstemons is **showy penstemon (P. speciosus).** It has elongate, blue-green leathery leaves; tall (up to 3 feet) coarse stems; and bright blue, bilaterally symmetrical flowers that are as much as 2 inches long. It is most common in Washington, Oregon, California, Nevada, and southwestern Idaho. A very similar and equally large and attractive species is **blue penstemon (P. cyaneus),** a conspicuous plant in the sandy sagebrush plains of eastern Idaho and adjacent Wyoming and Montana. A third tall, large-flowered species with bright blue flowers is **mountain penstemon (P. alpinus)** occurring in the high plains and mountains of the Great Basin and adjacent Colorado.

A very common penstemon of sandy plains and partially stabilized dunes in the steppes of northern Nevada and adjacent California, Oregon, Washington, and southwestern Idaho, is **sand penstemon (P. acuminatus).** This is a medium-sized plant (½ to 2 feet tall) with thick and leathery, blue-green, mostly basal leaves. Its flowers are bright blue to blue-purple, less than 1 inch long, bilaterally symmetrical, and

Scorched penstemon

congested in several whorls near the stem tip. The entire plant is often glutinous or sticky from epidermal exudation.

A frequent plant of dry, rocky (lithosol and talus) habitats more or less throughout the sagebrush steppe is **scorched penstemon (P. deustus).** This is a rather low, many-stemmed plant with whitish, lavender-striped or shaded, bilaterally symmetrical flowers which are approximately ½ inch long. The leaves are sharply toothed along the margins.

One of the most colorful penstemons is **firecracker penstemon (P. eatonii)** with its brilliant, crimson flowers which lack a landing platform and are pollinated by hummingbirds. This spectacular species is widespread in the high plains, open forests, and mountain ridges of central Ne-

vada, Utah, and the southern Rockies. It is most frequently found on talus slopes.

Two species similar in form and habitat requirements but very different in geographic distribution are **rock penstemon (P. gairdneri)** and **larchleaf penstemon (P. lariciflorus).** Both are low, many-stemmed plants with narrow leaves and pale lavender, bilaterally symmetrical flowers that are ½ to ¾ inch long. Both grow in dry, rocky (lithosol) sites, rock penstemon in Washington, Oregon, and adjacent Idaho and larchleaf penstemon in the eastern steppeland.

An attractive species with rather limited distribution, occurring along talus slopes in central Washington and Oregon, is **cut-leafed penstemon (P. richardsonii).** This is a tall (up to 3 feet), weak-stemmed plant

Firecracker penstemon

Larchleaf penstemon

Rock penstemon

Cut-leafed penstemon

with deeply divided leaves and bright lavender flowers which are ¾ to 1 inch long and are conspicuously inflated at the throat.

A highly variable and attractive species of wide distribution, occurring more or less throughout the steppeland, is **crested penstemon (P. eriantherus).** This is a low, hairy plant with rather elongate, usually toothed leaves. The showy flowers are 1 inch long or longer and vary in color from pale lilac or orchid to deep purple. It occurs in sandy-loam or clay soils, usually associated with sagebrush.

Two attractive, small-flowered species of rocky, talus slope habitats are **talus penstemon (P. pruinosus)** and **Great Basin penstemon (P. fremontii).** Both have deep blue or blue-lavender flowers which are sendom more than ½ inch long. Talus penstemon is a many-stemmed plant with toothed leaves and is common in the Washington steppe. Great Basin penstemon is a few-stemmed somewhat larger flowered plant which is relatively common in the Great Basin area.

Dwarf monkey flower (Mimulus nanus) —The name *Mimulus* is derived from the Latin *mimus* meaning mimic, especially mimic actor. Presumably the flowers of *Mimulus* with their "grinning face" mimic monkeys.

There are a number of small annual species of *Mimulus* in the steppes and deserts of North America including both yellow- and red-flowered forms. All have showy irregular (bilaterally symmetrical) flowers with a basal tube and spreading petal lobes, the lower three forming a landing platform for

Crested penstemon

Great Basin penstemon

Talus penstemon

Dwarf monkey flower

nectar-seeking pollinators. In the dwarf monkey flower, the flowers are deep magenta with dark red and yellow markings in the throat of the tube. Also in the throat are two longitudinal ridges covered with short, yellow hairs.

In many sandy or fine-gravelly sites, especially in basaltic areas such as the Craters of the Moon National Monument in Idaho, this plant forms very dense populations with a spectacular display of color. It is most common in southern Idaho, Nevada, and eastern Oregon. It flowers in early summer.

Yellow monkey flower (Mimulus guttatus)—The yellow monkey flower is an extremely variable species, both in size and geographical distribution. It occurs most frequently in the mud and gravel of slow moving water in small streams. Here it is a tall, showy perennial, often associated with watercress. It also occurs occasionally in seepage areas along rock ledges. In this habitat it exists mostly as a small, few flowered annual, an adaptation which enables the plants to complete their life cycle very quickly. The population survives in the form of seeds during dry periods when the seepage stops. In the spring the dense population provides a spectacular display of brilliant yellow and red color.

Yellow monkey flower is rather succulent with opposite, heavily veined and toothed leaves. The flowers are irregular (bilaterally symmetrical) with five yellow petals which are fused at the base into a tube. The three lower petals provide a landing platform for nectar-seeking bees. The platform is marked

Yellow monkey flower

with bright red splotches (hence the name *guttatus* which means spotted) and near the throat of the tube are numerous short, pollen-gathering hairs.

The yellow monkey flower is found in suitable habitats throughout the mountainous areas and high plains included within the sagebrush steppe.

Indian paintbrush (Castilleja species) —Certainly, no other inhabitants of the sagebrush steppe are as striking as the crimson Indian paintbrushes. Although the flowers are rather small and non-showy, they are associated with numerous colorful bractlike leaves that function as an attractant, thus aiding in pollination which is accomplished, at least in large part, by hummingbirds. The petals are fused into a narrow, elongate, greenish-red tube which

may or may not extend beyond the bracts. The sepals are partially fused and are colored similarly to the bracts. All paintbrushes are perennials with rather woody, well branched root systems. Most plants are covered with stiff hairs.

An interesting adaptation of paintbrushes is that they are able to parasitize the roots of associated plants, especially sagebrush. From the host plant, the paintbrush derives both water and organic materials, thus increasing its tolerance to dry conditions and its ecological range.

Several species of paintbrush are native to the sagebrush steppe, many very similar and difficult to distinguish. Some of the most common are: 1) **desert paintbrush (Castilleja chromosa)** — variable in color from brilliant crimson to shades of red, orange,

Desert paintbrush

or yellow, even within a single population. This is the most widespread paintbrush, occurring more or less throughout the sagebrush steppe except in Washington. 2) **narrow-leafed paintbrush (Castilleja angustifolia)** — also variable in color but frequently with a unique purplish-rose coloration by which it is distinguishable from other species. It is most common in Idaho, Montana, and Wyoming. 3) **mountain paintbrush (Castilleja applegatei)** — a crimson or red paintbrush which extends from the high plains into the mountains of eastern Oregon, southern Idaho, Nevada, Utah, and Wyoming (see the cover photo). 4) **linear-leafed paintbrush (Castilleja linariaefolia)** — a spectacular crimson-colored species of the eastern steppe and mountains (Great Basin area). This is the State Flower of Wyoming. 5) **Thompson's paintbrush (Castilleja thompsonii)** — a non-colorful plant with greenish-yellow bracts. It is the most widespread species in the steppe of Washington.

All species tend to favor the deeper, sandy soils, possibly because of similar requirements of host plants such as sagebrush.

Owl-clover (Orthocarpus species) — With casual observation, species of *(Orthocarpus)* can easily be mistaken for closely related Indian paintbrushes. Both have rather inconspicuous tubular flowers which are partially hidden among often colorful, bractlike leaves. However, paintbrushes usually are more colorful and are perennials, with thick, woody roots. Owl-clovers are all small annuals, less than 12 inches

Desert paintbrush

Desert paintbrush

Desert paintbrush

Linear-leafed paintbrush

tall. Also in *Orthocarpus,* the tube formed by the fused petals is two-lipped; the upper lip is often hooked forward and hoodlike, the lower lip is usually saclike and has three minute, toothlike projections.

There are a number of species of *Owl-clover* in the sagebrush steppe, particularly in the western "half." All prefer somewhat sandy sites and are usually associated with sagebrush. The two most attractive species are **Orthocarpus barbatus,** with yellow-green bracts and yellow flowers and **O. tenuifolius,** with conspicuous pink petal-like bracts and yellow flowers. The most widespread species are the golden-yellow-flowered **O. luteus** and the white-flowered **O. hispidus.**

Narrow-leafed paintbrush

Thompson's paintbrush

Owl-clover (O. tenuifolius)

Owl-clover (O. barbatus)

BROOMRAPE FAMILY (Orobanchaceae)

Broomrape (Orobanche fasciculata) — This is a very unusual and interesting plant which completely lacks chlorophyll and is thus non-photosynthetic. Its clustered stems are rather thick and fleshy with small, scale-like leaves and several, 2-6 inch flowering stalks, each with a single irregular (bilaterally symmetrical) flower. The stems, leaves, and flowers are yellow to purplish and are covered with sticky, glandular hairs. The petals are fused into a slightly-arched tube with five lobes. The root is fleshy and bulbous.

This and other species of broomrape are completely dependent upon associated plants for food, nutrients, and water. Because of their parasitic habit, they have been able to extend their range into areas for which they would otherwise not have been adapted. For example, *Orobanche fasciculata* does not possess adaptations relating to water preservation but depends on its host, sagebrush, for a constant source.

A somewhat similar but shorter plant with more numerous flowers is **Orobanche californica,** also usually parasitic on sagebrush. Both of these broomrapes are widespread in the steppe but are never common and are seldom observed because of their inconspicuous coloration.

Broomrape

PLANTAIN FAMILY (Plantaginceaae)
Hairy plantain (Plantago patagonica)—
This is a small woolly annual which seldom grows to be more than 6 inches tall. The long and narrow leaves are all borne at the base of the plant, the stems therefore being leafless. Although the flowers are by no means showy, this plant has a certain attractiveness with its long woolly hairs and white, widely-spreading, papery petals "nestled" among the hair of the spike. Also, an interesting evolutionary trend is reflected by the floral structures; this and other species of plantain are evolving from an insect-pollinated condition with showy flowers to a wind-pollinated condition with reduced, non-functional petals and long stamens which extend beyond the confines of the flower parts.

Hairy plantain is distributed along the western part of the sagebrush steppe, from British Columbia to California. It grows mostly in dry sandy areas or mildly alkaline sites. It is a frequent invader of disturbed areas, especially those subjected to excessive grazing pressures which tend to eliminate competitive grasses.

Hairy plantain

SUNFLOWER FAMILY (Compositae)

Matchbrush (Gutierrezia sarothrae) — Matchbrush is a low, unattractive shrub which is nevertheless conspicuous because of the dense populations it often forms and because it flowers during late summer after most steppe species have become dormant. The brittle, extensively branched plants are seldom more than 1½ feet tall and bear many very narrow leaves, usually slightly more than 1 inch long, the lower ones soon drying and falling off. The few, minute ray and disc flowers are borne in small heads which themselves occur in a branched, terminal, flat-topped inflorescence.

Under natural conditions, matchbrush tends to be more or less restricted to non-productive rocky habitats of dry sagebrush plains; however, with overgrazing it invades areas of better soil. When food is scarce, livestock feed on matchbrush which causes various and multiple intestinal disorders, abortion, production of weak offspring, and occasionally death. The species is prevalent in all our western states.

Rabbit brush (Chrysothamnus nauseosus) — Rabbit brush is an extremely common plant which rivals sagebrush in its distribution and ecological importance. Frequently they occur together as codominants of steppe communities and occasionally rabbit brush forms rather pure stands. However, it has a more restricted ecological range than sagebrush, requiring somewhat moister conditions and sandier soils.

Rabbit brush may also be mistaken for sagebrush — both being medium-sized shrubs with gray, woolly pubescence (hairs).

Matchbrush

However, rabbit brush lacks the strong sage odor and has narrow and non-lobed leaves. Most importantly, however, rabbit brush has more colorful, yellow disc flowers which are congested into showy clusters of small heads. The name "chrysothamnus" is of Greek derivation and means golden (yellow) shrub ("nauseosus" means heavy-scented). The fruits (achenes) are capped with numerous bristles which aid in seed dissemination.

A second, common species of rabbit brush is **Chrysothamnus viscidiflorus** which lacks woolly pubescence, is thus greener in coloration, and has somewhat sticky stems and flowers. Both species are distributed more or less throughout the sagebrush steppe and often occur together. Both provide poor quality browse for jackrabbits, deer, antelope, and other range animals.

Dwarf goldenweed (Haplopappus acaulis—Dwarf goldenweed is an attractive member of a rather large and variable genus, including both shrubs and herbs. It is a woody-based cushion plant with a stout taproot and a branched rootcrown giving rise to several short and erect, nearly leafless stems, each bearing a single showy head. The leaves are small and narrow (mostly less than 2 inches long), rigidly erect, and crowded at the base of the plant forming a dense mat. The yellow heads have approximately eight to ten colorful rays and several disc flowers. The few rays per head distinguish this and other goldenweeds from the similar yellow daisies.

Dwarf goldenweed is common and widespread in the steppe, being absent only in

Dwarf goldenweed (H. acaulis)

Washington where it is replaced by **Haplopappus stenophyllus.** It occurs in very dry, rocky sites in the plains and along open ridges. The very attractive goldenweed **Haplopappus armerioides** is similar to dwarf goldenweed but is larger in all aspects. The two closely related species overlap in distribution and have similar habitat requirements.

Townsendia or daisy (Townsendia species)—The similarities between species of *Townsendia* and those of *Erigeron* (all daisies) are much more impressive than are the differences. It is extremely difficult to distinguish between the two genera without reference to technical characteristics. However, the species of *Townsendia* usually have larger heads and shorter flowering stalks, the heads often occurring at ground level. As is typical of most daisies, the heads consist of inner, non-showy disc flowers and outer, colorful rays.

Probably the two most common plains species are **T. florifer** and **T. parryi,** both shortlived plants with taproots. *Townsendia florifer* has several flowering stems, each with a single head of pastel-pink rays. The leaves have rather long petioles and elliptical blades. This species occurs more or less throughout the steppe and is usually associated with sagebrush. *Townsendia parryi* is a lower plant with fewer stems and larger heads. The rays are lavender to blue, large and attractive. This species also has wide distribution but is particularly common in southwest Montana.

Aster (Aster species)—As a group, asters are distinguished by a *combination* of

Dwarf goldenweed (H. armerioides)

Daisy (T. parryi)

Daisy (T. florifer)

relatively few blue, pink or white rays (usually with fewer than 25 per head); leafy, branched stems with several heads; and a flowering period of mid to late summer. With some exceptions, including the three described below, the asters which occur in the steppe are weedy roadside species.

Chilian aster (Aster chilensis)—a highly variable, creeping, leafy-stemmed plant with several rather small heads. The rays are pale blue to pink or sometimes white. This typical aster is common in the high plains and dry mountain ridges of western North America. It flowers in midsummer.

Woody-rooted aster (Aster xylorrhiza) — a daisylike cushion plant with many mostly basal leaves and large heads with white rays. It occurs in somewhat moist, lowland sites in the plains of the Great Basin. It flowers in early summer.

Lava aster (Aster scopulorum)—a low plant with few to several stems, each bearing a single head. The rays are blue-violet, usually eight in number, and approximately ½ inch long. The leaves are also about ½ inch long, are narrowly elliptical, and are crowded along the middle of the stem. The lava aster grows in dry, rocky (lithosol) sites in northern Nevada and parts of Idaho and Oregon. It flowers in early summer.

Daisy (Erigeron species) — The many colorful daisies constitute an ecologically important and conspicuous element of the steppe vegetation. Most species have the typical daisylike floral design consisting of showy heads with inner, usually yellow, disc flowers and numerous narrow blue or pink to purple (or occasionally white or yellow)

Woody-rooted aster

Lava aster   Thread-leafed daisy

outer rays. Rarely the rays are absent. Most daisies have several erect flowering stems —which seldom exceed 15 inches in height —each bearing a single head. The many narrow and elongate leaves occur predominantly toward the base of the stems. The steppe daisies flower in spring or early summer.

Many species of *Erigeron* occur in the mountains and plains of western North America, most in non-forested areas with well-drained sandy or gravelly soils. A closely related group of species in the genus *Townsendia* occur in similar habitats and are easily mistaken for members of *Erigeron*.

One of the most common and widespread daisies is **thread-leafed daisy (Erigeron filifolius)** which gets its name from its lin-

ear leaves. This is an extensively branched plant which forms rather large, symmetrical clumps. It has numerous heads with blue or pink rays. It occurs most frequently in sandy areas, sometimes on dunes, and is distributed in the western part of the steppeland from Canada to California and Nevada and extends eastward to the plains of Wyoming.

A common and very distinctive, white-hairy daisy is **shaggy daisy (E. pumilus).** This species has rather small heads with white, or occasionally pale pink or blue, rays. It occurs in dry sandy soils and is distributed throughout the steppeland.

Within the steppelands of Wyoming, Colorado, and Utah, the most common daisy is the low, white-flowered **plains daisy (E. engelmannii)** which is most prevalent in dry, thin or gravelly soils. The leaves are

Shaggy daisy

Plains daisy

Linear-leaf daisy

narrow, elongate, and primarily basal. The heads are small, usually less than an inch across, with many white rays and yellow to orange disc flowers.

Linear-leaf daisy (Erigeron linearis) is a common and attractive yellow-flowered plant which frequently forms dense populations on lithosol or talus sites. This is a cushion plant with narrow basal leaves and numerous short upright flowering stems. It occurs in the western "half" of the sagebrush steppe.

An unusual and drought-tolerant species of the southern steppe and adjacent desert is **ray-less daisy (E. aphanactis).** This widespread species is distinctive among the daisies because of a lack of rays. It is attractive, however, with its numerous bright yellow disc flowers. Like most daisies, it inhabits sandy or rocky areas.

A showy daisy occurring in sandy or rocky habitats in eastern Washington, Oregon, and western Idaho is **cushion daisy (E. poliospermus).** This is a low, few-stemmed species with colorful purple to violet rays.

In the southern part of the steppeland, **foothills daisy (E. argentatus)** can be found. It is an attractive plant with pale ("soft") lavender rays. It occurs in high, sandy, sagebrush plains and extends upward into piñon-juniper woodlands where it is often found on fine-textured talus slopes.

A very common daisy on rocky mountain ridges is **dwarf mountain daisy (E. compositus).** This is a low, hairy plant with pale blue to lavender rays. It is unlike other daisies in that its leaves are segmented at the tips.

Ray-less daisy

Cushion daisy

Rabbit brush (C. Nauseosus)

Plains lupine, eastern Washington

Rosy everlasting (Antennaria rosea) —
There are a number of species of everlasting
(Antennaria) but none are as widespread,
as showy, nor as variable as rosy everlasting which is a low, mat-forming plant that
spreads by runners. The leaves are small,
numerous, and mostly crowded on very
short shoots. The flowering stems are erect,
up to 12 inches tall, and have several narrow leaves and a dense cluster of small
heads which resemble the toes of a kitten,
hence the frequently used common name
"pussy toes." Each head has many very
small, unisexual flowers and is surrounded
by thin and papery, white to rose red, attractive bracts. The stem and leaves are densely
woolly giving the entire plant a grayish
coloration.

The rosy everlasting is common in the
high sagebrush plains of the Rocky Mountains and eastern Cascades from Canada
to California and New Mexico. It extends
upward in open pine and Douglas fir forests
and may reach the Alpine Zone on dry,
rocky ridges. Its bracts tend to be more
colorful (redder) in mountainous habitats.
Throughout its range, it flowers in early
summer.

Balsamroot (Balsamorhiza species) —
The sunflowerlike balsamroots (Gr. *balsama*
= balsam, *rhiza* = root) are among the
most colorful associates of sagebrush in the
high plains. In the spring their bright "sunny faces" provide a brilliant array of yellow
color over broad expanses of the sagebrush
steppe. They are distinctive plants with
rather large heart-shaped or divided basal
leaves and several leafless (or nearly so)

Rosy everlasting

flowering stems, each with a single large head (2-4 inches across) bearing showy, outer rays and numerous inner disc flowers. The roots are thick and carrotlike, though somewhat woody, and although they have a rather bitter, balsamlike flavor, they have a history of having been eaten by plains Indians.

There are a number of more or less morphologically distinct but genetically similar species that frequently hybridize when they overlap in distribution. The most common and widespread species is **arrow-leafed balsamroot (Balsamorhiza sagittata)** which has arrowhead-shaped leaves that are as much as 12 inches long and half as wide and are covered with fine woolly hair which gives them a grayish color. This plant occurs mostly in deep, sandy soil and ex-tends from the steppe upward into open, ponderosa pine forests and sagebrush dominated ridges in the mountains. Another common balsamroot of Washington and Oregon is **B. careyana** which is probably more drought tolerant than B. sagittata from which it can be distinguished by its more heart-shaped, non-woolly leaves.

Other common steppe balsamroots have deeply lobed or divided, more elongate leaves. These include **rock balsamroot (B. hookeri)**—a low plant with numerous basal leaves, leafless stems, and attractive heads (2-3 inches across)—which occurs in dry rocky (lithosol) habitats more or less throughout the steppeland; **Rocky Mountain balsamroot (B. incana)**—a slightly larger but similar plant which requires more moisture; and **large-leaf balsamroot (B.**

Arrow-leafed balsamroot

Large-leaf balsamroot

Rock balsamroot

Dwarf sunflower

macrophylla)—a robust, more montane species of Idaho, Wyoming, and Utah.

Dwarf sunflower (Wyethia amplexicaulis)—In the high "moist" plains and foothills of the sagebrush steppe, few species can match the color and panoramic beauty of the dwarf sunflower. In many respects it resembles the closely-allied balsamroots and overlaps with them in distribution. However, the dwarf sunflower is easily distinguishable by a combination of the following characteristics: 1) the leaves are elliptical and occur on the stem as well as at the base of the plant; 2) there are usually two or more heads per stem, the central one larger than the others; 3) the plant is totally hairless and has a bright, varnished appearance, especially the green, resinous bracts (involucre) at the base of the heads.

The showy heads of the dwarf sunflower have the typical combination of outer, petal-like ray flowers and inner disc flowers, both types similarly yellow colored. In respect to the uniformly colored heads, *Wyethia* resembles balsamroots and differs from many other sunflowerlike plants.

Dwarf sunflower occurs in sandy loam or gravelly sites, sometimes with sagebrush but often in more moist, meadowlike areas. It has a very wide range and can be found in suitable habitats throughout the steppe-land. The genus was named in honor of Nathanial Wyeth, early 19th Century western North American explorer.

Blepharipappus (Blepharipappus scaber)—Although this species has apparently never been given a widely accepted common name, it is widespread and rather

Blepharipappus

attractive. The representative plants are small, usually branched, narrow (linear)-leaved annuals which vary in height from a few to several inches depending on growth conditions. As with other members of the sunflower family, the flowers are borne in heads, one to several per plant. Each head has two to eight ray flowers with conspicuous, wedge-shaped, three-lobed, white, petallike rays, and approximately five central disc flowers, also white. The plants are found most frequently in loose, somewhat sandy soils and are widely distributed in the western part of the steppe-land, extending east to central Idaho and Nevada.

A closely related, similarly distributed plant is **Layia glandulosa,** which differs from **Blepharipappus** in having somewhat broader and often toothed leaves, very abruptly narrowed rays, and yellow rather than white disc flowers.

Oregon sunshine (Eriophyllum lanatum)—Oregon sunshine is a very attractive plant with bright golden-yellow flowers and whitish-woolly leaves. The plants are usually low and often cushionlike but may be as much as 2 feet tall. In any case they have several stems, each with one or few showy heads consisting of rather conspicuous green outer bracts (involucral bracts), six to fourteen rays and several disc flowers. The leaves—from which the species is named (Gr. *erio* = wool, *phyllum* = leaf; *lanatum* also refers to wool, the name therefore being redundant)—are usually cut into narrow segments but are sometimes nondivided or toothed (entire) and are long and slender.

Layia glandulosa

Oregon sunshine

Oregon sunshine can be found in a variety of habitats but most frequently occurs in dry sandy plains or on fine talus slopes. It is widespread in the steppeland and extends upward onto dry rocky sites in forest openings and ridges. It flowers in late spring or early summer.

Chaenactis (Chaenactis douglasii) — Chaenactis is a variable and common biennial or short-lived perennial with stiffly erect stems and long narrow taproots. The leaves are finely divided and fernlike, and are largest and most numerous near the base of the stem. Usually, the plants are somewhat woolly or glandular-sticky or both. Each plant has few to several heads borne singly at the ends of slender branches. The small tubular flowers are white to pinkish, and are densely congested in the heads. Unlike most members of the sunflower family, chaenactis does not have outer ray flowers, but the disc flowers, although small, are rather attractive.

Chaenactis grows in dry, sandy or gravelly sites, where it is rather inconspicuous, and can be found more or less throughout the sagebrush steppe. It extends upward onto open rocky ridges in mountainous areas.

Orange sneezeweed (Helenium hoopesii)—Because of the unusual orange coloration of its heads and its tall (1½-3 feet) stems, the orange sneezeweed is conspicuous in its surroundings. The stems are usually clustered and branched, and have a number of elongate, strongly veined leaves. The showy heads may be as much as 3 inches across and have orange or yellowish

Chaenactis

Orange sneezeweed

rays and disc flowers.

Although this species has a wide distribution—ranging from southeastern Oregon through Nevada and Utah to Colorado and Wyoming—it seldom forms very dense populations but is represented by scattered individuals. It is most prominent on mountain ridges and in open forests but extends downward onto high moist sagebrush plains.

Helenium is an ancient Greek name given to some plant, presumably in honor of Helen of Troy. The common name relates to its hay fever-producing capability. This and related plants are poisonous to livestock.

Blanket-flower (Gaillardia aristata) — The blanket-flower can easily be recognized by its distinctive heads. Each head bears approximately twelve attractive wedge-shaped rays which have three prominent lobes, are yellow with a purplish base, and average about 1 inch in length. The center of the head is brownish-purple. The plants are rather tall (up to 3 feet) with few to several stems, each bearing a single head and a number of elongate leaves, the upper ones usually toothed or lobed.

This species has a wide range and frequently grows as a roadside weed where it often forms dense populations. In the sagebrush steppe it can be found in the moister plains and dry meadows. It has frequently been cultivated as an ornamental garden plant and under non-competitive conditions grows very well.

Yarrow (Achillea millefolium) — Few species have been as successful in adapt-

Blanket-flower

Yarrow

ing to such a wide variety of habitat types as has yarrow. Its ecological success is attributable to the evolution of a number of ecotypic races or "environmental specialists." Representative races can be found in almost all general habitats from the desert to the alpine tundra, excepting forests and wet areas. It also has a wide geographical distribution and occurs throughout the sagebrush steppe.

The individual plants are usually somewhat more than 1 foot in height and often have several stems. The leaves are very finely divided and fernlike; the lower leaves have petioles and are longer than the upper, non-petiolate ones. The flowers are minute and are clustered into small, white heads each with three to five rays. The heads are congested into a flat-topped to rounded, umbrellalike cluster.

One of the most outstanding characteristics of yarrow is its odor, particularly when the leaves are crushed. The dried leaves also have a "minty" taste and are frequently used for flavoring, as in tea. Yarrow also has a long history of medicinal use and was named after Achilles who presumably used extracts from the plant to treat the wounds of his soldiers.

Gold star (Crocidium multicaule)—The gold star is a small, slender annual, seldom more than 6 inches tall, with one or more erect stems, each bearing a single head. The leaves are mostly basal (being reduced upward on the stem), often toothed, and have a tuft of hair in their axils. The generic name is derived from the Greek *crocid* which means loosely woven cloth or wool

Gold star

and relates to the woolly hair in the leaf axils. The bright golden-yellow rays are usually eight in number, and are ¼ to ½ inch long. The central, disc flowers are also yellow. As the seeds (achenes) mature, the receptacle becomes elongate and cone-shaped.

Although the plants are small and not particularly showy individually, they often occur in very dense populations providing a spectacular display of bright color at a time, early in the spring, when very few steppe species are yet flowering. The distribution of gold star follows the sagebrush plains and open forests on the east side of the Cascade Range in Oregon and Washington.

Foothills arnica (Arnica sororia)—The arnicas are distinct from most related members of the sunflower family in that they have opposite (paired) rather than alternate leaves. Also, most of the several species of western arnicas occur in subalpine and alpine habitats thus making *A. sororia* somewhat exceptional with its foothills and high plains distribution.

Foothills arnica has typical, bright yellow, sunflowerlike heads with outer rays and inner disc flowers. The solitary stems are 1-2 feet tall, with one head (rarely more) and two or three pairs of small opposite leaves. The basal leaves are much larger and more numerous than the stem leaves, and have conspicuous parallel veins.

Although it often invades meadows, foothills arnica is most frequently found in rather dry, gravelly soils of sagebrush communities, in regions where the winters are

Foothills arnica

Nipple-seed

cold and the springs are moist. It is widely distributed in southern and eastern Idaho, the high plains of Wyoming, and much of northern Utah and Nevada (the Great Basin).

Nipple-seed (Thelysperma subnudum) —This is one of the most beautiful of the many sunflowerlike plants of the sagebrush steppe. It has bright golden-yellow rays surrounded by attractive green bracts which are fused at the base to form a cup-shaped structure with triangular lobes. The lobes are unusual in having white, papery edges which contrast with the green of the bracts and the yellow of the ray and disc flowers. The plants have one or more, 4-12 inch stems, each bearing a single showy head. The basal leaves are divided into long and narrow (linear) segments. The reduced stem leaves are opposite and mostly undivided.

Thelysperma is a Greek word meaning nipple-seed and relates to the many minute, nipplelike projections coating the wall of the seed. *Subnudum* is descriptive of the almost nude (leafless) stem.

Nipple-seed occurs in very dry rocky or gravelly habitats in the hills and plains of the southern Rockies, from Wyoming through Utah and Colorado to Arizona and New Mexico. It is probably most common in open juniper woodlands where it flowers in early summer.

Groundsel (Senecio species)—*Senecio* is a very large genus with many species in western North America, most occurring in mountain meadows or on montane talus slopes. Although somewhat daisylike in

Gray groundsel

appearance, groundsels are generally characterized by having several rather small yellow heads all borne near the tip of the stem and of nearly equal height, thus giving the plant a flat-topped appearance. In most cases the heads contain both ray and disc flowers.

Probably the two most widely distributed groundsels of the sagebrush steppe are **gray groundsel (Senecio canus)** and **western groundsel (S. integerrimus).** Gray groundsel is an attractive plant with several 6-18 inch stems bearing many bright yellow heads. The leaves are grayish-woolly, at least on the underside. The several basal leaves are non-toothed (an unusual trait among the groundsels) and have elliptical blades with long petioles. The stem leaves are reduced, the upper ones becoming bractlike. This species is common in the high plains and extends well up into the mountains along open ridges.

Western groundsel is a much taller and coarser plant with one or few stems derived from a shallow fibrous root system. It is an extremely variable plant of high plains and mountains and is especially common in sagebrush communities of northeastern California.

Species of *Senecio* contain poisonous alkaloids but are sufficiently unpalatable that livestock poisoning seldom if ever occurs.

Horse brush (Tetradymia glabrata) — This is one of three similar and closely-related species that are widely distributed in the dry lands of western North America. All are small to medium-sized shrubs which

Western groundsel

Horse brush

119

closely resemble rabbit brush (Chrysothamnus) but usually occur in drier sites. In some areas — especially in southern Idaho, Wyoming, Nevada, and Utah—horse brush becomes a major dominant forming extensive and dense populations.

The stems of horse brush are brittle and usually whitish with short, dense woolly hairs, these sometimes occurring only in lines. The numerous leaves are small, narrow, and sometimes spinelike **(Tetradymia spinosa).** The flowers are bright yellow but small and occur with numerous bristles in groups of four in small heads.

Although essentially non-palatable and thus rarely eaten, horse brush is highly poisonous. The toxic principles are expressed in two ways, liver injury and photosensitization or sensitivity to light. In the latter case, a pigment from horse brush gets into the peripheral circulatory system and in light colored animals (especially white sheep) causes acute "sunburn" and extensive swelling around the head and neck. In extreme cases death may result from a combination of liver injury and sun damage.

Prairie pink (Lygodesmia grandiflora) —Most plains species of the sunflower family have either disc flowers or yellow rays (or both). Prairie pink is therefore distinctive in lacking disc flowers and having pink to lavender-blue rays. The plants are 4-12 inches tall with thin flexuous stems. (Gr. *lygos* = pliant or limber twig; *desmia* = bundle and relates to the frequently clustered stems). The leaves are very narrow (linear) and are reduced in size upward on the stems. Each stem has one or few heads

Prairie pink

False dandelion

with six to twelve showy rays of equal length (1-2 inches long).

Prairie pink occurs on gravelly hills and in sandy plains east of the Continental Divide in Wyoming, Colorado, and Utah. It flowers in early summer and sometimes forms large and beautiful populations.

False dandelion (Agoseris glauca) — This species has a number of variant forms and occurs in non-forested areas from the sagebrush plains to alpine meadows. It is also widespread geographically, being distributed throughout western North America.

As the common name implies, *Agoseris glauca* is dandelionlike in appearance. It has slender (more so than dandelion), erect, leafless stems, each with a single head of bright yellow rays which sometimes turn pinkish with age. The seeds (achenes) are parachutelike when mature and are scattered widely by the wind. The leaves are all basal and are narrowly lance-shaped or occasionally divided like those of dandelions. The tissue when torn exudes milky juice. Unlike the dandelion, *Agoseris* is not an aggressive weed and we therefore think of it as being more attractive.

The rather bitter milky juice solidifies into a rubberlike material which can be chewed as gum. This seems to have been a rather common trait of some of our plains Indians.

Hawk's-beard (Crepis species) — Because species of *Crepis* rather closely resemble the ubiquitous dandelion, their beauty is often not appreciated. Most steppe species are rather tall plants (up to 2 feet) with branched stems and showy, dandelion-like heads of yellow ray flowers. The seeds

Hawk's-beard (C. acuminatus)

Hawk's-beard (C. barbigera)

(achenes) are also similar to those of dandelion with their "parachutes" which aid in wind dissemination. The leaves are usually deeply divided into narrow, pointed segments, and most are borne at the base of the stem.

Three of the most common of several steppe species are **Crepis acuminatus**—widely distributed in the northern and higher plains; **C. atribarba**—also very widely distributed; and **C. barbigera,** common in Washington, Oregon, and eastern Idaho and probably of hybrid origin. All three species grow in somewhat sandy to coarse gravelly soil, and all flower in early summer.

Microseris (Microseris troximoides) — This is an occasional but widespread plant which in many respects resembles the common dandelion. It has a leafless stem with a single head of bright yellow, dandelion-like flowers. Each of the seeds (or more accurately fruits or achenes), has a "parachute" which aids in wind dissemination. The leaves are woolly-gray, narrow and straplike, and have wavy edges. The roots are mostly unbranched.

Although microseris is a rather attractive plant, the heads close early in the day, especially during hot weather, and the plant then becomes inconspicuous and non-showy. It is most frequently found in dry, somewhat sandy soil, more or less throughout the sagebrush steppe. It flowers early in the spring.

Microseris

KEY FOR THE IDENTIFICATION OF REPRESENTATIVE FAMILIES

Although the attempted use of an identification key may be a frustrating experience for the botanical novice, familiarity with the key and with plant structures in general should resolve most difficulties. Knowledge of plant structures can be supplemented by reference to the descriptive illustrations (page 131) and glossary (page 136). Familiarity with the key can be gained only through experience.

The key presented here is dichotomous or two-branched; that is, at every position in the key, the user has two mutually exclusive choices, "a" and "b" of the same number. In the identification of a plant, the user should start at the beginning of the key, and always progress forward (never backward), choosing only between the two descriptions ("a" and "b") of each numerical set until the selected choice refers to a family and page where the species of that family are pictured and described in the text. A few helpful notes in the utilization of this key are: (1) the choice must be between the "a" and "b" of the same number. (2) The descriptions of "a" and "b" should be read *carefully* before making a choice. (3) The two choices are sometimes separated in the key.

1a. Fragrant shrubs with twisted and gnarled stems; leaves wedge-shaped with three shallow or deep lobes; coloration gray-green from a dense covering of minute, woolly hair. . . . .**Sagebrush (Artemisia species)** page 17.

1b. Plants with various characteristics but not in the same combination as above.

  2a. Leafless, green shrubs with stiffly erect and jointed, broomlike branches; flowers not produced. . . . .**Ephedra family (Ephedraceae)** page 20.

  2b. Plants having green leaves OR otherwise not as above.

    3a. Plants spiny and leafless, thick and succulent, round and unbranched or branches flattened and jointed; flowers showy. . . . .
. . . .**Cactus family (Cactaceae)** page 72.

    3b. Plants not spiny OR otherwise not as above.

      4a. Non-green (brownish) parasitic plants with low, fleshy, clustered stems and scalelike leaves. . .**Broomrape family (Orobanchaceae)** page 100.

      4b. Plant with green leaves although these *sometimes* very small and/or covered with whitish hair.

        5a. Flowers densely congested into heads with greenish outer bracts, the heads sunflower- or daisy-like (with outer ray flowers and inner disc flowers), dandelionlike (with only ray flowers), or chaenactislike (with only disc flowers). See the illustrations. . . . .
. . . .**Sunflower family (Compositae)** page 102.

        5b. Flowers not in heads OR, if so, then the heads not as above (go to 6).

6a. Trees or large shrubs (two feet tall or more); flowers not blue.

  7a. Medium-sized, spiny shrubs with clustered, unisexual, mostly inconspicuous flowers. . . . .**Goosefoot family (Chenopodiaceae)** page 38.

  7b. Plants not spiny; flowers often conspicuous.

    8a. Leaves and branches opposite; flowers showy with four white petals. . . . . . .
. . . .**Syringa family (Hydrangeaceae)** page 55.

    8b. Leaves and branches alternate; flowers not showy OR if so, petals 5.

      9a. Trees or large shrubs with entire (non-toothed or lobed) leaves (including quaking aspen, a tree with white bark). . . . .
. . . .**Willow family (Salicaceae)** page 32.

      9b. Shrubs with toothed or lobed leaves.

        10a. Leaves lobed and maplelike in outline; sepals more showy than petals. . . . .**Currant family (Grossulariaceae)** page 56.
        10b. Leaves toothed or shallowly lobed but hardly maplelike; petals more showy than sepals. . . . . . .**Rose family (Rosaceae)** in part page 58.

6b. Herbs or small shrubs (mostly less than two feet tall); flowers *sometimes* blue.

11a. Grasslike herbs with hollow, joined stems and long, narrow leaves with parallel veins; flowers reduced and not obvious. . . . . **Grass family (Gramineae)** page 21.

11b. Stems and leafs NOT BOTH as above; flowers *usually* obvious when present.

12a. Sepals and petals 3 each, similar in size and color (the style branches flattened and petal-like in iris); leaves mostly basal, long and narrow (sometimes round) with parallel veins; plants not woody.

13a. Stamens 6; ovary superior; plants producing bulbs. . . . .
. . . . **Lily family (Liliaceae)** page 25.

13b. Stamens 3; ovary inferior; plants not producing bulbs. . . . .
. . . . **Iris family (Iridaceae)** page 30.

12b. Sepals and petals *usually* more than 3 each and seldom similar in size and color (if so, plants woody at the base); leaves various but *usually* not as above.

14a. Petals 4; flowers regular (radially symmetrical), usually showy.

15a. Stamens 8 (4 of the 8 sometimes shorter and poorly developed); flower parts usually borne on a long, narrow tube from the top of the ovary (ovary inferior) . . . .
. . . . **Evening primrose family (Onagraceae)** page 74.

15b. Stamens 4 or 6; flower parts borne on the receptacle, at the base of the ovary (ovary superior).

16a. Stamens 4; petals small and papery; flowers borne in a dense spike. . . . . **Plantain family (Plantaginaceae)** page 101.

16b. Stamens 6; petals *mostly* showy and not papery; flowers borne in racemes.

17a. Leaves palmately compound; stamens extended well beyond the petals. . . . . **Caper family (Capparidaceae)** page 51.

17b. Leaves not palmately compound; stamens *usually* not extended beyond the petals. . . . .
. . . . **Mustard family (Cruciferae)** page 47.

14b. Petals more or less than 4 (sometimes none); flowers *sometimes* irregular (bilaterally symmetrical) and sometimes inconspicuous (go to 18).

18a. Flowers inconspicuous; plants spiny OR white woolly. . . . .
. . . . **Goosefoot family (Chenopodiaceae)** in part page 38.

18b. Flowers usually conspicuous OR if not, plants neither spiny nor white woolly.

19a. Petals 6, white and showy; plants prickly. . . . .
. . . . **Poppy family (Papaveraceae)** in part page 46.

19b. Petals not 6 OR if so, NOT white; plants *usually* not prickly.

20a. Petals and sepals 3 each; flowers *usually* borne in umbels or heads; plants *usually* woody at the base. . . . .
. . . . **Buckwheat family (Polygonaceae)** page 34.

20b. Petals and sepals more or less than 3 each; flowers not borne in umbels or heads OR if so, petals 5 and plants not woody.

21a. Upper leaves (or bracts) and sepals reddish or yellowish, more showy than the petals. . . . .
. . . . **Figwort family (Scrophulariaceae)** in part page 42.

21b. Upper leaves green, not otherwise conspicuously pigmented (go to 22).

22a. Flowers clearly irregular (bilaterally symmetrical).

23a. Stamens more than 10; sepals blue, showy and with a single spur. . . . .
. . . . **Buttercup family (Ranunculaceae)** in part page 44.

23b. Stamens 10 or fewer; sepals green or reddish.

24a. Flowers sweet pealike; leaves pinnately or palmately compound; stamens 10. . . . . **Pea family (Leguminosae)** page 6.

24b. Flowers not pealike; leaves *rarely* compound; stamens 5 or fewer.

25a. Flowers pansylike; plants prostrate with divided leaves. . . . .
. . . .**Viola family (Violaceae)** page 70.

25b. Flowers not pansylike; plants taller OR if not, leaves not divided.

26a. Bushy shrubs with a strong minty odor; ovary developing into 4 nutlets . . . .**Mint family (Labiatae)** page 90.

26b. Herbs or *odorless* shrubs; ovary developing into a many-seeded capsule. **Figwort family (Scrophulariaceae)** page 92.

22b. Flowers regular (radially symmetrical).

27a. Stamens numerous, far more than 10 per flower.

28a. Flowers orange to red-orange; stamens fused at the base forming a tube.
. . . .**Mallow family (Malvaceae)** page 69.

28b. Flowers sometimes reddish but not orange; stamens not fused.

29a. Flowers pink, petals more than 5. . . . .
. . . .**Purslane family (Portulacaceae)** page 41.

29b. Flowers not pink OR if so, petals 5.

30a. Flowers blue to purplish OF if yellow (buttercups) then plants prostrate. . . . . . .**Buttercup family (Ranunculaceae)** page 44.

30b. Flowers yellow to reddish; plants erect.

31a. White-stemmed plants with sandpaperlike leaves. . . . . . .
. . . .**Loasa family (Loasaceae)** page 71.

31b. Plants neither white-stemmed nor with sandpaperlike leaves. . . . .**Rose family (Rosaceae)** page 58.

27b. Stamens 10 or fewer (go to 32).

32a. Leaves all basal (borne at ground level); petals reddish and turned backward, away from the face of the flower. . . . .**Primrose family (Primulaceae)** page 79.

32b. Leaves and flowers various but not combined as above.

33a. Petals fused into a tube with 5 lobes (more or less trumpet-shaped), all separating from the flower as a unit; stamens borne on (and inside) the petal tube.

34a. Erect plants with opposite leaves and slightly irregular, blue flowers.
. . . .**Figwort family (Scrophulariaceae)** page 92.

34b. Flowers clearly regular and not blue OR if blue, leaves either alternate or plants more or less prostrate.

35a. Stamens extending well beyond the petals, giving the flower clusters a bristly appearance. . . . .
. . . .**Waterleaf family (Hydrophyllaceae)** page 84.

35b. Stamens included within or barely visible beyond the petal tubes.

36a. Plants *usually* bristly hairy; flowers *usually* borne in a coiled cluster; style not branched; ovary developing into 4 nutlets.
. . . . **Borage family (Boraginaceae)** page 87.

36b. Plants not bristly hairy; flowers not borne in a coiled cluster; style 3-branched; ovary developing into a capsule . . . .
. . . .**Phlox family (Polemoniaceae)** page 80.

33b. Petals not fused (sometimes absent), separating from the flower individually; stamens borne on the receptacle or ovary.

37a. Tall (2-3 feet) slender herbs with colorful, sky-blue flowers. . . . .
. . . .**Flax family (Linaceae)** page 68.
37b. Shorter plants with reddish, purplish, yellow, or white flowers.
    38a. Flowers borne in umbels; leaves divided and carrotlike. . . . .
    . . . .**Parsley family. (Umbelliferae)** page 77.
    38b. Flowers not borne in umbels OR if apparently so, leaves not carrotlike.
        39a. Low succulent plants with star-shaped, yellow flowers. . . . .
        . . . .**Stonecrop family (Crassulaceae)** page 52.
        39b. Plants not *both* succulent and yellow-flowered.
            40a. Plants more than one foot tall with leafy stems and showy pink
                (or white) flowers. . .**Geranium family (Geraniaceae)** page 67.
            40b. Plants not having the same combination as above.
                41a. Dense cushion plants (not more than a few inches tall);
                    flowers white. . .**Pink family (Caryophyllaceae)** page 43.
                41b. Plants not as described above.
                    42a. Sepals 2; plants rather fleshy with pink flowers and a
                        pair of opposite stem leaves. . . . .
                    . . . . . .**Purslane family (Portulacaceae)** page 41.
                    42b. Sepals 5; plants not as described above.
                        43a. Leaves divided or lobed, mostly basal. . . . .
                        .**Saxifrage family (Saxifragaceae)** page 53.
                      43b. Leaves entire, neither divided nor lobed. . . . . . .
                        .**Sandalwood family (Santalaceae)** page 33.

APPENDIX II

Sagebrush steppe species listed by vegetative zone in which they most frequently occur. Some species occur regularly in two or more zones and therefore have multiple inclusions.

Standard-Type Zone

Achillea millefolium
Agropyron spicatum
Agoseris glauca
Allium acuminatum
Allium douglasii
Allium textile
Amsinckia retrorsa
Antennaria rosea
Arabis divaricarpa
Arabis holboellii
Arenaria hookeri
Argemone platyceras
Arnica sororia
Artemisia tridentata
Aster chilensis
Aster xylorrhiza
Astragalus bisulcatus
Astragalus crassicarpus
Astragalus miser
Balsamorhiza careana
Balsamorhiza incana
Balsamorhiza macrophylla
Balsamorhiza sagittata
Blepharipappus scaber
Brodiaea douglasii
Brodiaea howellii
Brodiaea hyacinthina
Bromus tectorum
Calochortus lyallii
Calochortus macrocarpus
Calochortus nuttallii
Castilleja angustifolia
Castilleja applegatei
Castilleja chromosa
Castilleja linariaefolia
Castilleja thompsonii
Chaenactis douglasii
Chrysothamnus nauseosus
Chrysothamnus viscidiflorus
Clarkia pulchella
Claytonia lanceolata
Clematis hirsutissima
Cleome lutea
Collomia grandiflora
Collomia linearis
Comandra umbellata
Crepis acuminatus
Crepis atribarba
Crepis barbigera
Crocidium multicaule
Cryptantha glomerata
Delphinium geyeri
Delphinium nuttallianum
Dodecatheon pauciflorum
Elymus cinereus
Ephedra viridis
Erigeron aphanactis
Erigeron argentatus
Erigeron compositus
Erigeron engelmannii
Erigeron filifolius
Erigeron poliospermus
Erigeron pumilus
Eriogonum compositum
Eriogonum heracleoides
Eriogonum ovalifolium
Eriogonum strictum
Eriogonum umbellatum
Eriophyllum lanatum
Erysimum asperimum
Festuca idahoensis
Fritillaria pudica
Gaillardia aristata
Geranium viscosissimum
Geum triflorum
Gilia aggregata
Grayia spinosa
Gutierrezia sarothrae
Hedysarum boreale
Helenium hoopesii
Hesperochiron pumilus
Hydrophyllum capitatum
Layia glandulosa
Lithophragma bulbifera
Lithospermum ruderale
Lomatium dissectum
Lomatium gormanii
Lomatium grayi
Lomatium triternatum
Lupinus ammophilus
Lupinus argenteus
Lupinus caudatus
Lupinus greenei
Lupinus leucophyllus
Lupinus sericeus
Lupinus wyethii
Lygodesmia grandiflora
Mertensia longiflora
Microseris troximoides
Oenothera tanecetifolia
Opuntia polyacantha
Orobanche fasciculata
Orthocarpus barbatus
Othocarpus hispidus
Orthocarpus luteus
Orthocarpus tenuifolius
Oxytropis sericea
Penstemon alpinus
Penstemon cyaneus
Penstemon eriantherus
Penstemon fremontii
Penstemon speciosus
Perideridia gairdneri
Phacelia adenophora
Phacelia hastata
Phlox longifolia

Phlox multiflora
Phlox speciosa
Plantago patagonica
Poa sandbergii
Populus tremuloides
Potentilla gracilis
Purshia tridentata
Ranunculus glaberrimus
Salsola kali
Senecio canus
Senecio integerrimus
Sisymbrium altissimum
Sisyrinchium angustifolium
Sisyrinchium douglasii
Sisyrinchium inflatum
Sphaeralcea coccinea
Sphaeralcea munroana
Stanleya pinnata
Tetradymia glabrata
Tetradymia spinosa
Thelypodium laciniatum
Thelysperma subnuda
Townsendia florifer
Townsendia parryi
Wyethia amplexicaulis
Zygadenus venenosus

Lithosol Zone

Arenaria hookeri
Artemesia rigida
Aster scopulorum
Astragalus purshii
Balsamorhiza hookeri
Erigeron engelmannii
Erigeron linearis
Erigeron poliospermus
Eriogonum caespitosum
Eriogonum sphaerocephalum
Eriogonum thymoides
Gutierrezia sarothrae
Haplopappus acaulis
Haplopappus armerioides
Haplopappus stenophyllus
Lewisia rediviva
Linum perenne
Lomatium gormanii
Lupinus aridus
Opuntia polyacantha
Pediocactus simpsonii
Penstemon deustus
Penstemon gairdneri
Penstemon lariciflorus
Phlox hoodii
Phoenicaulis cheiranthoides
Poa sandbergii
Ranunculus glaberrimus
Sedum lanceolatum
Trifolium macrocephalum
Viola trinervata

Sand-Dune Zone

Arenaria franklinii

Astragalus succumbens
Blepharipappus scaber
Calochortus macrocarpus
Chaenactis douglasii
Chrysothamnus nauseosus
Chrysothamnus viscidiflorus
Cleome lutea
Comandra umbellata
Cryptantha flava
Cryptantha leucophylla
Erigeron filifolius
Erigeron pumilus
Eriogonum niveum
Eriogonum ovalifolium
Erysimum asperimum
Layia glandulosa
Linum perenne
Lupinus argenteus
Lupinus sericeus
Mimulus nanus
Oenothera deltoides
Oenothera pallida
Oenothera trichocalyx
Opuntia polyacantha
Orthocarpus barbatus
Orthocarpus luteus
Oryzopsis hymenoides
Penstemon acuminatus
Penstemon speciosus
Phacelia hastata
Phacelia linearis
Phlox speciosa
Plantago patagonica
Purshia tridentata
Rumex venosus
Salsola kali
Stipa comata

Talus Zone

Amelanchier alnifolia
Arabis holboellii
Argemone platyceras
Artemisia tridentata
Balsamorhiza sagittata
Ephedra viridis
Erigeron argentatus
Eriogonum compositum
Eriogonum niveum
Eriogonum ovalifolium
Eriophyllum lanatum
Gilia aggregata
Haplopappus armerioides
Heuchera cylindrica
Leptodactylon pungens
Lesquerella douglasii
Lomatium dissectum
Lupinus sulphureus
Mentzelia laeviculmis
Oenothera brachycarpa
Oenothera caespitosa
Penstemon alpinus
Penstemon deustus

Penstemon eatonii
Penstemon fremontii
Penstemon pruinosus
Penstemon richardsonii
Philadelphus lewisii
Phlox multiflora
Physaria didymocarpa
Physaria vitulifera
Purshia tridentata
Ribes aureum
Ribes cereum
Salvia dorrii
Stanleya pinnata
Thelypodium laciniatum
Thelysperma subnuda

Meadow Zone

Camassia quamash
Dodecatheon pauciflorum
Iris missouriensis
Mimulus guttatus
Potentilla gracilis
Sisyrinchium angustifolium
Sisyrinchium douglasii
Sisyrinchium inflatum
Thermopsis montana

Saline Zone

Distichlis stricta
Elymus cinereus
Eurotia lanata
Grayia spinosa
Salsola kali
Sarcobatus vermiculatus

COMPLETE FLOWER

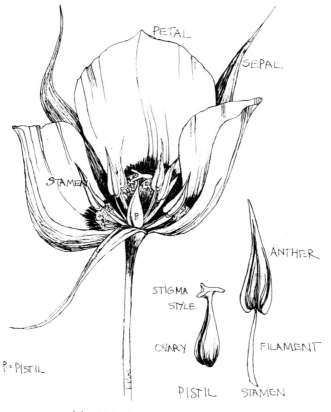

PETAL

SEPAL

STAMEN

P

ANTHER

STIGMA
STYLE

OVARY

FILAMENT

P = PISTIL

PISTIL   STAMEN

MARIPOSA LILY

ADDITIONAL CHARACTERISTICS
ILLUSTRATED:

SUPERIOR OVARY
REGULAR FLOWER
RADIAL SYMMETRY
NON-FUSED PETALS

PRIMARY INFLORESCENCE TYPES

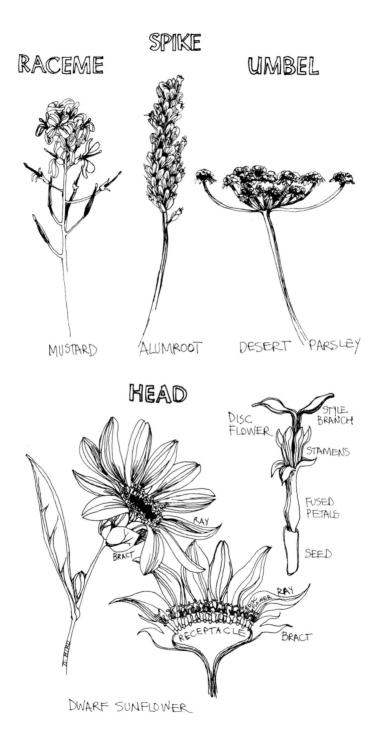

RACEME

SPIKE

UMBEL

MUSTARD

ALUMROOT

DESERT PARSLEY

HEAD

DISC
FLOWER

STYLE
BRANCH

STAMENS

FUSED
PETALS

SEED

RAY

BRACT

RAY

DISC
FLOWER

RECEPTACLE

BRACT

DWARF SUNFLOWER

RADIAL SYMMETRY

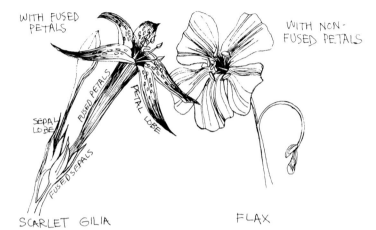

WITH FUSED PETALS

WITH NON-FUSED PETALS

FUSED PETALS

PETAL LOBE

SEPAL LOBE

FUSED SEPALS

SCARLET GILIA

FLAX

BILATERAL SYMMETRY

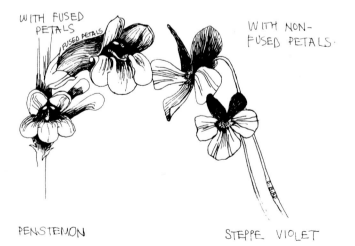

WITH FUSED PETALS

FUSED PETALS

WITH NON-FUSED PETALS.

PENSTEMON

STEPPE VIOLET

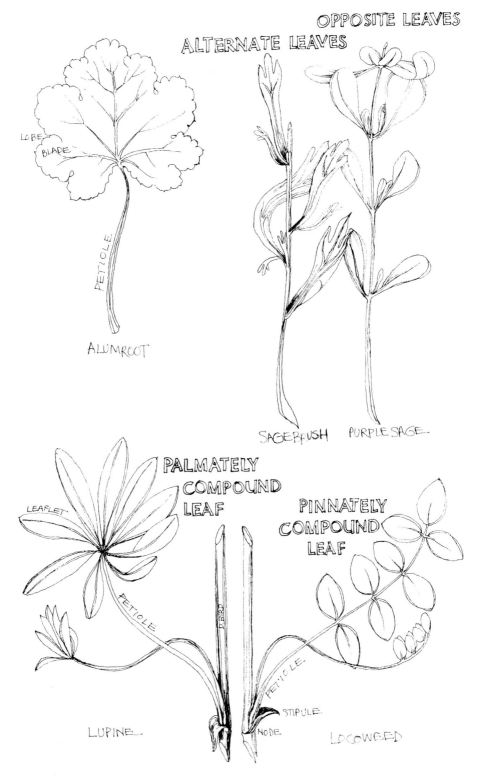

OPPOSITE LEAVES

ALTERNATE LEAVES

LOBE

BLADE

PETIOLE

ALUMROOT

SAGEBRUSH   PURPLE SAGE

PALMATELY
COMPOUND
LEAF

PINNATELY
COMPOUND
LEAF

LEAFLET

PETIOLE

T.BIRD

PETIOLE

STIPULE

LUPINE   NODE   LOCOWEED

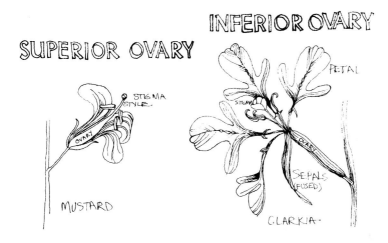

SUPERIOR OVARY

STIGMA
STYLE.
OVARY

MUSTARD

INFERIOR OVARY

PETAL
STIGMA
OVARY
SEPALS
(FUSED)

CLARKIA.

GLOSSARY

Achene — A small, hard, one-seeded fruit which functions as a single seed.

Alkaline—Basic as opposed to acidic; high pH.

Alkaloid — A toxic nitrogen-containing substance. Numerous different alkaloids are produced by plants and serve a defensive role, being poisonous to animals.

Alternate—As applied to leaves; not opposite, one leaf per node (see the illustrations).

Annual — A plant that lives only one year (from seed to seed in one year).

Axil—The angle formed by a leaf with the stem.

Basal—As applied to leaves: at the base of the stem, at or near ground level.

Biennial—A plant that lives two years, the first year producing leaves and a thick taproot, the second year developing an erect stem with flowers.

Bilaterally symmetrical — Relating to a flower: irregular, with a left side and right side; mirror images can be produced *only* by dividing the flower in a vertical plane; one (or more) of the petals and/or sepals is (are) unlike others (see the illustrations).

Blade—The flat part of a leaf or petal (see the illustrations).

Bract—A small modified leaf usually occurring at the base of flowers or flower clusters.

Bulb — A thickened, fleshy structure which usually occurs below ground and functions in food storage and reproduction (as an onion bulb).

Capsule — A fruit which becomes dry and splits open at maturity shedding its seeds; usually it contains two or more compartments.

Clasp—To appear to grasp the stem as some leaf blades that partly or totally encircle the stem.

Community—A group of organisms (plants) living together in a given habitat.

Coniferous — Adjectival form of conifer (a cone-bearing, usually evergreen gymnosperm).

Cushion—A form of growth of some plants, dense and low in stature, resembling a cushion.

Deciduous—Falling away, as leaves falling off at the end of the growing season.

Disc flower—One of the central flowers of a head of a sunflower, daisy, etc.; a tubular-shaped flower lacking a flattened extension (see the illustrations).

Dissemination — The act of spreading or scattering such as seeds or pollen in the wind.

Dominant—One of the most important plants of a given community because of numbers and/or size; a plant which has a major effect on other plants of the community.

Elliptical — Longer than wide with similar ends (not egg-shaped); a squashed circle.

Elongate—Much longer than wide.

Fleshy — Rather thick and succulent; containing juices (water).

Flexuous—Limber, easily bent.

Follicle — One of two or more capsulelike fruits produced by a single flower; a dry fruit which splits open at maturity and contains a single compartment and a single row of seeds.

Glandular — Having glands which secrete resinous, often sticky material.

Habitat—The home of a given plant, unique in having a particular set of environmental conditions.

Head — A dense cluster of flowers which lack stalks; the inflorescence of a composite or member of the sunflower family (see the illustrations).

Herb—A plant lacking a hard, woody stem.

Inferior—As related to an ovary: the flower parts borne on (above) the ovary or conversely, the ovary borne below (and inferior to) the flower parts (see the illustrations).

Inflorescence—A flower cluster.

Irregular — As related to a flower: one or more of the petals and/or sepals being unlike the others; bilaterally symmetrical (see the illustrations).

Leaflet—One of the leaflike segments of a compound leaf (see the illustrations).

Lithosol—Literally, rock-soil; a rocky, thin-soil habitat as in basaltic (lava-flow) areas.

Linear—Long and very narrow, with parallel sides.

Lobed—As related to a leaf: cut or dissected with rounded outer parts.

Mat-forming — Low, dense, and spreading horizontally, resembling a mat or carpet.

Nocturnal — Active at night; as applied to flowers, open at night and closed during the day.

Nodding — As related to a flower: hanging with the face of the flower downward.

Nutlet—One of four or more hard-shelled, one-seeded fruits.

Oblong—Longer than wide.

Opposite—As related to leaves: paired at the nodes; two leaves per node (see the illustrations).

Oval—Broadly elliptical; slightly longer than wide.

Ovary — The seed-containing part of the flower; the part of the flower that matures into a fruit (see the illustrations).

Ovate—Egg-shaped.

Palmate—Shaped like the palm of the hand with extended fingers.

Palmately compound—As related to leaves: divided to the midvein in such a way that the leaflets are borne at the same point and spread like fingers.

Parasite—Growing on and deriving nourishment from another living plant.

Pedicel—The stalk to a flower or fruit (see the illustrations).

Perennial—A plant that lives more than two years, it may die down to the roots each year but sprouts up the next.

Petal—One of the bractlike segments of the inner whorl of flower parts usually colored or showy (see the illustrations).

Petiole—Leaf stalk (see the illustrations).

Pinnate—Featherlike, with a central axis and perpendicular projections.

Pinnately compound—As related to leaves: divided to the midvein with the leaflets arranged on both sides of the extended axis of the petiole (see the illustrations).

Pistil—The central (female) part of the flower containing the ovary, style, and stigma (see the illustrations).

Pubescence — General term for hairiness, woolliness, etc.

Raceme—An elongate, unbranched flower cluster, each flower having a stalk or pedicel.

Ray—The bladelike extension of a ray flower (see the illustrations).

Ray flower—One of the outer flowers of a sunflower, daisy, etc. that has a flattened, elongate, colorful extension (see the illustrations).

Regular—As related to a flower: each petal (and sepal) similar to the other petals (and sepals); radially symmetrical (see the illustrations).

Rhizome—An underground stem that produces roots and upright branches (stems); an organ by which plants spread (such as quack grass and Canadian thistle).

Rootcrown—the juncture between the root and stem; the crown of the root.

Rootstalk—A rhizome.

Runner—A prostrate stem which roots at the nodes and produces erect branches (as with strawberries).

Saline—Salty, having sodium salts, potassium salts, etc.

Sepal—One of the bractlike segments of the outer whorl of flower parts, usually green (see the illustrations).

Shrub—A woody plant that branches at or near ground level.

Spike—An elongate flower cluster with sessile (nonstalked) flowers.

Spur—A hollow extension of a petal or sepal and often contains nectar.

Stamen—the pollen-containing part of the flower (see the illustrations).

Steppe — A nonforested region dominated by grasses and low shrubs.

Stipule — Leaflike or bractlike appendages at the base of the petioles of some leaves (see the illustrations).

Style—The narrow portion of the pistil, connecting the ovary with the pollen-receptive stigma (see the illustrations).

Succulent—Soft and juicy, filled with water.

Superior—As related to an ovary: the flower parts borne on the receptacle below the ovary (see the illustrations); conversely, the ovary above (superior) to the other flower parts.

Talus—Loose gravel or boulders on a slope.

Taproot—An elongate, unbranched, vertical (carrotlike) root.

Umbel—An umbrella-shaped flower cluster (see the illustrations).

Unisexual—One sex as a staminate (male) flower or plant.

Whorl — A group of three or more leaves, flowers, petals, or whatever radiating from a single point such as a node (see the illustrations).

Woodland—An area dominated by widely-spaced trees of low stature, savannalike.

Greasewood on salt flat near Oregon-Nevada border

PHOTOGRAPHY

The photographic work in this book is an attempt to blend scientific integrity with aesthetic appeal. Authenticity is maintained in that each plant has been photographed in its natural habitat without the use of artificial backgrounds or additional lighting. On occasion it was necessary to allow scientific needs to have priority over artistic value in order to present an impression of the plant useful in identification of a species.

Readers familiar with the sagebrush steppe and who have tried photographing these plants recognize the frustrations of playing games with the incessant winds of midday. When slower film speeds and small apertures are combined the needed shutter speed is often in the one-eighth or one-fourth second range, and you wait patiently on bended knee for a momentary lull. Sometimes you even resort to incantations that may not be heeded by the wind, but give relief to your vexation.

The major equipment used in this photography was a Mamiya RB67 single lens reflex mounted on a tripod equipped with a low mount universal tilt head. The selection of lenses included focal lengths of 65, 90, 127 and 250 millimeters along with an assortment of extension tubes. The films used were Kodak's 120 Ektachrome Professional (ASA 50) and High Speed Ektachrome (ASA 160) held in interchangeable magazines that when attached to the camera's revolving back allowed either vertical or horizontal transparencies of 6 by 7 centimeters.

Occasionally bulky equipment such as this is not the most effective. The time required to set up for each picture may become excessive or the need to use very small apertures to ensure adequate depth of field results in shutter speeds too slow to prevent the blur of subject movement. Difficulties of this type may suggest the advisability of using small format 35 mm equipment where ease of operation results in faster setups and the availability of short focal length high speed lenses permits the retention of depth of field without the handicap of long exposure times. It is also likely that the photographic product needs to be a transparency that is easily projected. Here 35 mm has its great advantage.

The popularity of 35 mm single lens reflex (SLR) cameras with internal exposure meters is easily understood by those who augment their enjoyment and understanding of nature by recording their observations to be reviewed later or shared with others. A number of low-cost but effective accessories may assist in obtaining pictures that retain the observed details. First in importance is a tripod or similar device to help hold the camera stationary during exposure, since a characteristic of the SLR is vibration caused by the movement of mirror, aperture linkage and shutter. If carrying a tripod seems too cumbersome, a bean bag can be placed upon the ground or other solid object and formed to cradle the camera. Reduction in camera movement can improve photographic efforts much more than suspected. (See *Modern Photography,* January 1974, page 90.)

To increase image size beyond that obtainable with just the normal lens, extension tubes can be employed. Most extension tubes now retain the automatic diaphragm features of the camera, and the internal metering system eliminates the need to compute the effect of lens extension upon the effective aperture. One disadvantage of using extension tubes with the normal lens is that the camera must be held very close to the subject and it becomes difficult to avoid casting unwanted shadows. A solution in some cases is to use the extension tubes with a lens of longer focal length.

Another accessory that helps at times is a right angle viewfinder attachment. When the camera is on the bean bag at or near ground level, it may be difficult to position oneself to be able to see into the standard eyelevel finder without uncomfortable contortions.

It is not the intent here to present a course in the techniques of field photography, but only to encourage our readers to increase their employment of *Sagebrush Country* by generating their own photos of the beautiful flowers to be found in this land that is so often considered void of life by the casual traveler.

SPECIES	LOCATION	DATE

SPECIES	LOCATION	DATE

SPECIES   LOCATION   DATE

Editor:
Thomas K. Worcester

Design:
Robert Reynolds